CELTS

CELTS

THE HISTORY AND LEGACY OF ONE
OF THE OLDEST CULTURES IN EUROPE

MARTIN J. DOUGHERTY

amber
BOOKS

Published by
Amber Books Ltd
74–77 White Lion Street
London
N1 9PF
United Kingdom
www.amberbooks.co.uk
Appstore: itunes.com/apps/amberbooksltd
Facebook: www.facebook.com/amberbooks
Twitter: @amberbooks

ISBN: 978-1-78274-166-4

Project Editor: Sarah Uttridge
Designer: Jerry Williams
Picture Research: Terry Forshaw

Printed in China

Picture Credits

AKG Images: 22 (Interfoto), 111, 170 (Peter Connolly)

Alamy: 12 (David Newham), 15 (Skyscan), 23 (Imagebroker), 26 (DPA), 32 (AGE Fotostock), 35 (Hemis), 37 (AGE Fotostock), 49 (John Warburton-Lee), 59 (Chris Hellier), 70 (HIP), 75 (Alan King), 78 (David Robertson), 81 (Pictorial Press), 82 (Prisma Archivo), 94 (Classic Image), 96 (Adrian Sherratt), 97 (Andy Buchanan), 99 (Ancient Art & Architecture), 105 (Florilegius), 110 (Ivy Close Images), 112 (Keith Heneghan), 120 (Classic Image), 139 (Classic Image), 148 (Prisma Archivo), 154 (Clement Phillippe/Arterra), 157 (CM Dixon/HIP), 162 (Kevin George), 169 (Lanmas), 172 & 175 (Juan Francisco Jiminez Martin), 177 (Bertrand Reiger/Hemis), 180 (Adam Woolfitt/Robert Harding), 181 (CM Dixon/Ancient Art & Architecture), 192 (GL Archive), 198 (Krys Bailey), 200 (Tony Smith), 206 (Tony Watson), 211 (World History Archive)

Alamy/The Art Archive: 86, 90, 92, 93, 147, 153, 165

Alamy/Interfoto: 20, 25, 34, 76, 91, 117, 149, 152, 189

Alamy/David Lyons: 38, 39, 46, 107, 138, 216

Alamy/North Wind Picture Archive: 52, 73, 87, 174, 183, 188

Amber Books: 145, 151

Bridgeman Art Library: 160 (Musee des Antiquities Nationales)

Corbis: 28 (Elio Ciol), 41 (Alain Le Garsmeur), 58 (Adoc-Photos), 74 (Print Collector), 102 (Chris Hill/Ocean), 178 (Leemage), 194 (Tarker), 196 (Leemage), 218 (National Geographic Society)

Dorling Kindersley: 6 (Russell Barnett), 64 (Paul Hams), 137 (Russell Barnett), 140 (Eddie Gerald)

Dreamstime: 44 (Marbury67), 95 (Spumador), 114 (Mardyn), 125 (Luca Quadrio), 142 (Anzemulec), 164 (Peter Spirer), 185 (David Harding), 197 (Moreno Soppelsa), 207 (Andrew Emptage)

Mary Evans Picture Library: 16, 18, 21 (J. Bedmar/Iberfoto), 51 (English Heritage), 53, 56 (English Heritage), 66, 67 (JJJ), 69, 106 (Arthur Rackham), 118, 119, 122, 126, 127, 156, 204, 208, 212, 213, 214 (English Heritage), 215

Werner Forman Archive: 60 (Moravian Museum), 61 (National Museum, Prague), 80, 83 (Musee de Rennes), 84 (Musee des Antiquities Nationales), 89 (National Museum, Copenhagen), 104, 113 (National Museum of Ireland), 134 (National Museum, Copenhagen)

Werner Forman Archive/British Museum: 9, 29, 47, 68, 77, 85, 150, 176

Fotolia: 8 (Scrumsrus), 10 (John Braid), 33 & 42 (Antonio Alcobendas), 100 (Ian Woolcock), 109 (John Braid), 136 (Morrbyte), 158 (Calin Stan), 202 (Andreas J)

Fotolia/Erica Guilane-Nachez: 7, 14, 45, 55, 63, 65, 71, 101, 144, 159, 161, 171, 184, 195

Getty Images: 50 (Hulton), 146 (Danita Delimont/Gallo Images), 166 (Dagli Orti/De Agostini), 191 (Hulton)

Getty Images/Bridgeman Art Library: 17, 31, 62, 141

iStock: 128

Public Domain: 123, 167, 203

TopFoto: 131, 132

CONTENTS

INTRODUCTION

The Celts are a mysterious people whose history is shrouded in myth and misinformation. The latter stems largely from the fact that many of the Celtic people were opponents of the Roman Empire, and of course it was the victors that wrote the history books. Thus much of what we know about the Celts is distorted by Roman misunderstanding or misrepresentation, further coloured by later generations' veneration of Rome.

The fashion for all things classical in the eighteenth and nineteenth centuries led to the widespread belief that Ancient Greece and Rome were the source of all cultural virtue, and thus by definition the 'barbarians' that opposed these civilizations were filthy, uncultured savages who needed saving from themselves at the point of a sword. The image put forward in Roman writings is one of bringing the light of civilization to the dark and savage corners of the world, and since much of what Celts might have recorded about themselves was destroyed in the process this concept became the widely accepted version of events.

On the mainland of Europe, Celtic society was absorbed into the Roman Empire and changed enormously, while in the British

RIGHT: Celts spread across Europe from the Atlantic coasts to the Danube basin, and even into Asia Minor. Over such a large area, regional variations in their culture were inevitable, but a distinctive 'Celticness' can still be discerned.

Isles there were other influences that caused the Celts to change over time. Much of what we know about the Celts has been pieced together from fragmentary evidence or biased accounts, but one truth has emerged: they were anything but uncivilized.

Although today's popular view of the Celts is still influenced by the version accepted in the eighteenth and nineteenth centuries, we are beginning to understand these people a lot better, and to realize just how influential they were upon the course of European history. This is hardly surprising – the Celts were a widespread and numerous people who settled in much of Europe and the British Isles.

ABOVE: **Early interactions between Celts and Romans had profound consequences for the future of Europe. Had relations not broken down, leading to the sacking of Rome, history might have taken a very different course.**

Small wonder, then, that as the Roman Republic expanded its sphere of influence it came into contact with Celtic people. Relations were sometimes good, sometimes less so. It was a Celtic army that sacked Rome around 390 BCE, leading to a military revolution that ultimately created the all-conquering legions. It was Celts, usually referred to as Gauls by the Romans, who provided much of the resistance to Roman expansion in Europe. Without proud Gallic warriors on the opposing side, the glory of Rome might have shone less brightly. After all, glory is won by defeating worthy opponents… and the Celts certainly were that.

Survival of the Celts

The culture of the European Gauls was largely absorbed into that of the Roman Empire, and some elements were distorted or destroyed. However, this was a two-way street to some extent, and Celtic influences did find their way into the Roman culture. In areas that were less thoroughly Romanized, or which were not conquered at all, the Celtic way of life survived and was melded with other cultures. While the tongue of the Roman Empire, Latin, is a dead language, some Celtic languages are still spoken today.

The Roman Empire did not reach Ireland, and attempts to push into Scotland were fought to a standstill until the Empire ceased to expand. Tribes in the border region traded with Rome, generally via Roman Britain, and absorbed some elements of Roman culture while remaining independent. Beyond this border zone the Roman influence was much less, and Celtic society continued as it had for generations before.

The Celtic languages live on mainly in Scotland and Ireland, with significant numbers of speakers in Canada and some cities of the USA. They are minority tongues, but proudly clung to by their speakers as a symbol of independence and an honourable heritage.

Although the Celtic languages are diminishing, some elements of Celtic society have found their way into the mainstream of modern culture. Traditional folklore and even everyday practices have in some cases come from the Celtic people. It is possible that the habit of throwing coins into a fountain or pool for good luck is derived from a Celtic ritual, or from an even earlier era. Some traditional monsters and otherworldly spirits also bear a distinct resemblance to those of Celtic mythology.

Many place names in Europe are Celtic in origin, and have been inhabited since the heyday of Celtic culture. Often, once a settlement's pattern has been established it survives through subsequent rebuilding, with the general layout of streets and squares remaining roughly the same from the Iron Age. Thus in some towns and cities we can today walk the same paths as our ancestors, stopping to browse the wares of a market that has been held in the same square for hundreds of years. In wilder places, fragments of Celtic society still remain in the form of standing stones and monuments of long-ago forgotten events.

BELOW: The Celtic Cross is an important symbol of early Christianity. Once they adopted the new religion, the Celts were instrumental in spreading it, and in so doing helped shape the development of the early Church.

The Spread of Christianity

The Celts were also heavily influential in the spread of the Christian Church, and elements of their complex and fascinating mythology found their way into European Christian practice. It is easy to think of the Church as a monolithic structure whose ways are the same everywhere, but visiting a few old churches soon reveals that religion, like everything else, was heavily influenced by the characteristics of the people who first practised it.

Celtic designs and motifs are often found in churches, gravestones and monuments. These are the same symbols as were used by the pagan Celts, now co-opted by Christianity and part of its traditions. Similarly, once the Celtic people had adopted Christianity, they were enthusiastic in practising and spreading it to others. Many of the great religious figures during the early spread of Christianity came from Ireland and other Celtic regions.

Celtic zeal for Christianity took some believers very far from home. When Norse explorers discovered Iceland, they found a small community of Irish monks already living there. Upon realizing that the Vikings were moving in next door these monks, probably wisely, decamped. Their presence in Iceland is perhaps more remarkable than the arrival of the Norsemen; the latter were in the habit of sending out raiding and trading expeditions, and explored distant waters to find new lands. A land mass as big as Iceland was bound to be spotted sooner or later.

For a small group of monks to find Iceland and set up a community there represented far more individual effort than an entire culture of explorers eventually stumbling upon a large island. The colony on Iceland was a significant achievement, for all that it was eventually abandoned. Certainly the Celtic Christians put a lot of effort into their religious endeavours, and thus helped shape the future of the northern European Church.

Traders and Craftsmen

The Celts were also great traders. Goods have been found in remote parts of Scotland that originated on the Continent and were bought as part of a continuous trade network. The image of filthy barbarians in their squalid huts is at least challenged, if indeed it is not shattered, by the knowledge that these 'barbarians' were trading for decorative goods from half a continent away, and making both functional and beautiful items for use and trade.

ABOVE: This bronze-faced shield was found in the River Thames, London, where its wooden backing had rotted away leaving only the highly decorated front. It is likely that the shield was thrown into the river as a religious offering.

The Celts were great workers of metal, producing high-quality weapons and armour as well as decorative items of silver and gold. They were also excellent weavers, using sophisticated machinery to produce clothing that was more than merely functional. This level of economic activity was made possible by a stable society with laws and social rules that were enforced upon those that did not want to observe them.

Despite the success of Celtic society, much of what we know today has had to be pieced together from fragmentary or unreliable sources. Few of the Celts' own records survive, and accounts left by Greek and Roman scholars are – deliberately or otherwise – misleading in places. This may be partially a result of what amounts to propaganda, and partly because the scholars did not understand Celtic society.

Having seen the Celtic way of life only from the outside and on a fragmentary basis, Roman scholars were not in a position to write in an informed manner. Not only had they not experienced the Celtic way of life, but they also tended to see only those groups that were in contact or conflict with Rome. The inner workings of Celtic society were probably a mystery to their chroniclers, who made guesses or simply recorded what little they knew for certain.

BELOW: The Broch of Gurness in the Orkney Isles was constructed between 500 BCE and 200 BCE and is the best preserved of all Iron Age Broch villages. The settlement consisted of a central tower (Broch) and several dwellings, all surrounded by a system of defensive ditches.

Other evidence comes from archaeology, which has its own problems. We can know for sure that a sword buried with a Celtic chieftain was made in a certain manner, but we cannot do more than speculate about the details of his life. We can examine the clothing and shoes that have been found at archaeological sites, but the people who wore them cannot tell us what it was like to live their lives. Thus much of what we 'know' about the Celts is in fact inferred rather than known for certain.

> 'MUCH OF WHAT WE KNOW TODAY HAS HAD TO BE PIECED TOGETHER FROM FRAGMENTARY SOURCES.'

Much can be determined from building techniques and materials, and from the layout of houses and settlements, and a combination of common sense and archaeological expertise allows us to draw what are probably good conclusions from the things that have been found. But ultimately any reconstruction of an ancient society is based on what seems likely rather than what actually was. There is no way around this; our knowledge is built up of inferences based upon facts and cross-referenced wherever possible, but it remains a picture assembled from fragments of a jigsaw puzzle… and we cannot be certain that all of the fragments are from the same puzzle.

An Expansive Culture

Any study of the Celts is made more complex by the fact that their culture was spread over a great expanse of Europe and existed for centuries. During this time great events unfolded and changed all of the civilizations that were exposed to them. Thus statements that apply to one group of Celts at one time in one place may not be relevant elsewhere or at another time. Studies are often defined by the archaeological site with which they are connected. Different sites give snapshots of Celtic culture in that location, and through the similarities between these we can infer some underlying principles of the Celtic culture as a whole.

It is perhaps fitting that the Celts are so difficult to figure out; they were a complex and diverse people whose influence helped determine the course of European history and still has relevance today.

WHO WERE THE CELTS?

Looking back into history, we need to compartmentalize events and eras in order to make sense of them. Thus we try to create neat blocks of history built around clearly defined protagonists.

This is necessary to avoid information overload, and there are so many exceptions, special cases and complex situations that it is impossible to perceive the norm. As a result, many people know a few simple facts about the Celts and their society, and it is possible to assume that this is the whole truth. The reality, however, was anything but simple or clear-cut.

The question of who the Celts were is far more complex than at first it might appear. The name conjures up an image of a red-haired warrior people, whose men sported impressive moustaches and whose women were strong and somewhat formidable. They were the enemies of Rome, the builders of strange carved-stone monuments and worshippers of spirits that have remained part of popular folklore ever since. They were also instrumental in spreading Christianity throughout much of Europe.

OPPOSITE: The distinctive straw-thatched Celtic round house may seem primitive compared to Roman villas and Greek temples of the same era, but it was well-constructed, weatherproof and durable. It could be built or repaired with natural materials obtained locally.

BELOW: The popular image of the Celts is one of 'noble barbarians' who sported fearsome moustaches and loved to fight. This is only one small part of the story, however; the Celts were a complex and sophisticated people.

We know that the Celts were excellent workers of metal, fearsome warriors and capable of producing colourful, finely made clothing. They lived in round houses or hill-forts, and were organized into tribes that often warred among themselves. Yet much of this common perception is so general as to be virtually meaningless, and in some cases it is inaccurate or misleading. This is hardly surprising; when trying to encapsulate a culture that covered most of Europe and existed for centuries, a few sentences can give only the broadest of indications. As we begin to focus on the details of Celtic society, apparent contradictions begin to manifest themselves.

This, too, is only natural. The Celtic people of the British Isles or those that settled in what is now Turkey were subject to different cultural influences than those of Iberia and Gaul. The Celtic people of 800 BCE, at the beginning of the Iron Age, were different to those that spread Christianity after the fall of Rome. Such a vast expanse of distance and time is bound to encompass large changes in culture and society; what is surprising is not so much the similarities that remain as the fact that Celtic society remains recognizable as such throughout.

Defining Celtic History

Many cultures have a distinct start and end date, albeit one imposed by historians long after the fact. Usually there is an event that can be pegged as the start or the end of an era, such as the fall of a city or the rise of a new society. This is true of some segments of the Celtic world, but the Celts were so widespread that although distinctly Celtic society ended in some areas at a certain date, it continued elsewhere.

In truth, although it is possible to estimate a start date, there is no clearly defined end to the 'Celtic Era'. The Celtic people were marginalized or subsumed in some areas, and in others their identity was gradually absorbed into a new culture. Yet elements of Celtic society

still exist today in the form of languages still spoken and popular folklore that is still repeated. The Celts did not come to an end; they evolved as societies always do. This process is still going on today, and it was happening throughout the era in which Celtic societies were dominant in Europe.

People in the past did not live in a clearly defined era; they lived in a time they called 'now'. This era was subject to constant – if often slow – changes in culture, language and relations with other groups. Society might evolve slowly or be wracked by catastrophe and rapidly changed as a result. Different cultures and various genetic groups met and mingled, affecting and influencing one another. The result was continual change, and it is only by focusing tightly on a specific place and time that we can obtain a clear snapshot of what life was like in that particular 'now'.

As soon as the focus is expanded, in terms of both time and place, we must begin to generalize based on observed trends and situations that existed sufficiently long or in enough areas to be considered the norm. The more precise a detail, the more likely it is to belong only to a specific moment in time at a given

ABOVE: **The hill fort at Maiden Castle is one of the largest Iron Age fortifications ever discovered. Its complex system of banks and ditches dates from the La Tène period (around 450 BCE); before this the fort was significantly smaller and less well defended.**

place. That said, we can create some good working generalizations from our observations of the Celts, and so long as these are not taken to be the definite truth everywhere at every time, they will suffice for most purposes.

First Impressions

Around 400 BCE, a large group of 'barbarians' became known to the inhabitants of northern Italy. They were tall, fair- or red-haired people with loud voices, and they were sufficiently warlike to drive the local people, the Etruscans, from at least part of their lands. This brought the new arrivals to the attention of Rome, which was at that time only beginning its rise to greatness.

ABOVE: Around 400 BCE, a force of citizen-soldiers from Rome was decisively defeated at the River Allia by the Senones, a Celtic tribe. This was the beginning of an era of war between the Celts and the rising power of Rome.

Roman chroniclers found much to write about the new arrivals. Their clothing, consisting of a shirt and trousers with a cloak over the top, was well made and of bright colours, and their practice of spiking their hair with a mixture of lime and water gave these 'barbarians' a dramatically fierce appearance. This was compounded by an array of notable moustaches.

The newcomers were of impressive physical build and some were armoured with helmets and body protection. Others apparently chose to go into combat naked. Either way these were very powerful warriors and the Etruscans were soon pushed out of the Po Valley. They asked for help from their Roman neighbours, who sent envoys to the new arrivals.

Negotiations between the Roman envoys and the Celtic 'barbarians' were initially conducted in an atmosphere of mutual respect. The Celts recognized that if the Etruscans looked to Rome for military assistance, then Rome was clearly powerful. An agreement was plainly preferable to war, so the Celts offered what amounted to a land-for-peace deal. The Roman envoys challenged this on the grounds that it amounted to military extortion, but the Celtic point of view was clear – they had the might to make it happen, so they had the right to do it.

The Romans decided to assist their Etruscan neighbours, earning the enmity of the Celts who demanded justice for their slain warriors. Since the envoys were powerful in Roman politics, this was refused. Indeed, instead of being punished for breaking the 'law of nations' by taking sides after declaring neutrality as envoys, the perpetrators were promoted to high office.

The Celts then marched on Rome, which deployed six legions to oppose them. The legion of the time was modelled on the Greek style of warfare, with well-equipped hoplites in the centre and lighter troops on the flanks. Estimates of the date fall around 390–387 BCE, but there is more certainty about the outcome of the battle.

The two forces met at the River Allia, where the Celtic leader, Brennus, quickly divined the Romans' weakness. The Roman military system of the time was based on a militia in which men

BELOW: The Senones were able to force Rome to the brink of paying a vast tribute before they were driven from the city by a force under Marcus Furius Camillus. This required two days of bitter street fighting in Rome itself before the Celts were finally defeated.

had to provide their own equipment. The centre of the Roman line was a solid mass of spears and shields held by armoured men, but the ill-equipped troops of the flanks were an easier target.

A Celtic charge broke the flanking forces, some of whom fled to Veii and others to Rome. The centre force was then surrounded and overwhelmed, which robbed Rome of its best-equipped and experienced fighting men. Perhaps worse, these were the most powerful and affluent citizens; decision-makers and leaders were lost in the disaster at the Allia, leaving the way open for an attack on the city of Rome itself.

The Celts were able to storm the weakly held city without undue difficulty, although some Roman forces held out on the Capitoline Hill. Attacks on this position were beaten off, and the Celts agreed to withdraw if paid a huge bribe. Naturally, negotiations for payment broke down and a second Roman force reached the city. After inconclusive street fighting a field battle took place and this time the Celts were defeated.

The Celts were driven away from Rome, but they had left an indelible mark upon history. A massive reorganization of the Roman military was begun, moving away from the Greek style of warfare to a more flexible approach, and Rome was heavily fortified. It would be centuries before the city once again suffered invasion.

This assault upon Rome was carried out by just one Celtic tribe, the Senones, who warred with Rome on and off for another century before finally being defeated. The Roman

BELOW: According to legend, Roman guard dogs failed to raise the alarm when the Senones attacked the city at night, but the honking of geese alerted the defenders. Thereafter, dogs were punished in an annual ritual whilst geese were showered with honours.

name for the Senones and their fellow Celts was Galli, or Gauls, which essentially meant 'barbarians' but eventually came to refer to what we now call the Celtic people of Europe. As the Romans discovered when they tried to expand their territory northwards, there were a great many tribes of these Gauls and they had spread all across northern Europe in the preceding centuries.

Origins of the Celts

The name 'Celt' comes from the Greek Keltoi, which, like the Roman name for them, also means 'barbarians'. Exactly when the Ancient Greeks came into contact with the proto-Celts is open to speculation, but it is known that the Celtic people interacted with various Greek civilizations over a lengthy period. Sometimes Celts might be found serving as mercenaries in Greek wars and sometimes they fought against various Greek forces.

It is probable that interactions of some kind took place from at least as early as the end of the Greek Dark Age. This lasted from around 1200 to 800 BCE and followed the collapse of earlier Greek civilizations. The Greek Dark Age also coincided with the collapse of other societies in the Eastern Mediterranean region, resulting in a dearth of written records from that period.

The Bronze Age Collapse, as this period is known, saw the New Kingdom of Egypt, the Hittite Empire of Anatolia (Turkey) and the Mycenaean Greek kingdoms all succumb to some great disaster. The reasons remain obscure; causes have been suggested ranging from drought and natural disasters such as earthquakes and volcanoes to invasions by foreigners.

It is known that during the period of the Bronze Age Collapse (1200–1150 BCE), most of the cities on the eastern Mediterranean coasts were sacked and they were often destroyed. Fragmentary accounts refer to raids by the 'Sea Peoples', whose identity is unknown. There may have been a single source for these raids, or perhaps there was more than one group active. Similarly, the Bronze Age Collapse may not have had a single cause.

'"CELT"' COMES FROM GREEK KELTOI, WHICH, LIKE THE ROMAN NAME FOR THEM, ALSO MEANS "BARBARIANS".'

The Bronze Age Collapse had far-reaching consequences. Here, Ramses III of Egypt is depicted leading the defence of his kingdom against the mysterious Sea Peoples. The eradication of many established states may have opened the way for early Celtic expansion.

Greek legends also speak of the Dorian Invasion, or Dorian Migration, in which a people of unknown origins entered Greece from the north and took control of parts of the region. Exactly what form this 'invasion' took, and who the Dorians were, remains unknown, although there have been suggestions that this incursion was in part responsible for the collapse of Mycenaean civilization in Greece and the subsequent Dark Age.

Whether the ancestors of the Celts were involved in any of these events is not known, but a period of turbulence, including the collapse of three major civilizations, would have implications far across the Ancient world, and may have in part created the conditions for the rise of Celtic culture. It also suggests a troubled time in which the ability to defend would be as important as the ability to create and to build. This would have altered the path that Celtic society was developing along even if the Celts were not directly involved. This development can be traced back through preceding pre-Celtic and proto-Celtic societies, although their original point of origin is open to some debate.

European Bronze Age Culture

Around 1300 BCE, what is now known as the Urnfield culture emerged in central and eastern Europe. It is named for the burial practice of cremating the dead and placing their ashes in urns. Prior to this, the Tumulus culture of the preceding four centuries used burial mounds. As with all such transitions, the change was not immediate or sharply defined, but took place gradually over many years with both methods in use at the same time.

The Urnfield culture was widespread, covering much of Europe north of the Alps, from what is now France to the Danube basin. It was not unified of course; many local variations have been found. In many cases the style of pottery used by Urnfield people changes abruptly from one place to another, suggesting boundaries between tribes or cultural subgroups. However, a general culture can be discerned throughout the entire region.

Urnfield people raised cereal and vegetable crops, and kept domestic animals for meat and wool. They also had horses, but the horse of the era was small and not well suited to riding. Chariots and wagon-like conveyances were also used by the Urnfield people, who may have developed them independently or could have been influenced by chariot use of the Hittites. Chariots were probably symbols of high status and may have been used in war. They were at times buried with important (or at least wealthy) individuals.

The Urnfield people made leaf-shaped swords out of bronze. These were sufficiently well made to take and retain a cutting edge, and to remain useful after delivering several cutting blows. The transition from stabbing swords to cutting

swords took place around the time that the Urnfield culture replaced the Tumulus culture, but there is no real evidence of a concrete link between burial methods and weapon making. It seems likely that the move instead characterized a general improvement in metallurgy and smithing capability that allowed new styles of weapon to be made.

The slashing sword remained a popular and indeed characteristic weapon with later Celtic cultures; further evidence that the Urnfield period should be considered

BELOW: The Urnfield culture was characterized by the use of funerary urns like this one, to bury the ashes of the dead. Previously, the general practice was to bury the dead under a mound, or tumulus.

the beginning of Celtic society. Previous cultures were significantly different in many ways, but the Urnfield people show definite characteristics of later Celtic society.

During the Urnfield period, a society led by warriors was emerging. This may have been due to increased competition between groups as populations grew; those that could win wealth from others (or prevent it being taken by them) became more important to society than those who created or grew what it needed. Alternatively, perhaps the reason was more basic – those that bore arms and knew how to use them could force others to obey, and as prosperity increased society became able to support a warrior/ruler class or at least a group for whom warfare was a major secondary activity.

ABOVE: Although the Urnfield culture predated the widespread adoption of iron weapons, its military equipment was not primitive. Bronze weapons were well-made and at least the equal of the early iron alternatives.

Whatever the reason, the move towards a warrior-led society coincided with the establishment of hill-forts from around 1000 BCE onwards. Constructing a hill-fort required very significant effort and would not have been undertaken unless a real need was perceived. Since fortified settlements became common, it seems likely that this was a period of significant conflict.

Whether or not large-scale migration took place in this period as has been suggested by some historians, it is known that proto-Celtic people had reached Spain by about 1300 BCE and were active in northern Europe (modern-day France and Germany) by 1200 BCE. There is evidence that many hill-forts became centres for metalworking, and as techniques developed the smiths learned to work iron instead of (or as well as) bronze.

The move from bronze to iron was not instantaneous; indeed, there is evidence that some iron working may have taken place as early as 2000 BCE. By the fourteenth century BCE, the Hittites of Anatolia were making some goods from iron, but these were rare and precious; weapons and tools were made of bronze. Early iron weapons were no better than bronze; the move from bronze to iron may have been the result of necessity rather than preference.

Thus the Iron Age was not defined by the introduction of iron working, but the point where it became prevalent. This varies from place to place, but by around 800 BCE the people of central Europe were making extensive use of iron tools and weapons.

Iron Age Celts

Exactly how and when the proto-Celts became actual Celts as we know them is open to some debate. What is certain is that they will not have noticed the difference at the time – the evolution was gradual and possibly not even noticeable to those living in the era. Be that as it may, the Celts are normally considered to be

BELOW: **This replica of a Hallstatt-era burial shows some of the grave-goods interred with the deceased. Decorative or valuable items, and amphorae of wine, were commonly included in graves, as were weapons and armour.**

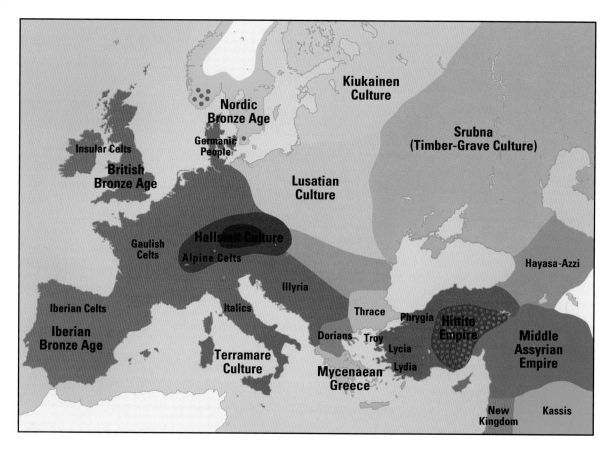

ABOVE: This map gives an indication of the main cultural traditions of various regions. The Celtic cultures that developed in Gaul, Iberia and the British Isles were similar in many ways, but were subject to different influences and thus had a number of distinct variations.

an Iron Age people, although how much of their culture resulted from the introduction of iron working and how much is due to coincidental development is open to conjecture.

By 800 BCE, the process of social evolution had created what is now known as the Hallstatt culture. This is named for an archaeological site at Hallstatt in Austria where many of the discoveries that defined this culture were made. The people of the Hallstatt region possessed a good metalworking industry before the switch to iron was made. It was only logical that their smiths would continue to export good weapons and tools, only now made of iron rather than bronze.

The Hallstatt culture was not completely unified of course. In more westerly areas it was common to bury leaders with a sword and sometimes in an ornate chariot burial, while in the east the axe seems to have been preferred as a leader's weapon and symbol of office, and burials in armour were more common. In both cases this indicates a significant level of prosperity;

grave goods might be much poorer if the living were short of weapons and the tools of war.

The Hallstatt culture, to a great extent, defines the early Celts, although they are not the only people who lived this way in the region. Other ethnic and social groups adopted a similar lifestyle as a result of cultural influences through trade and general interaction. Thus the Hallstatt culture can be taken as an example of the earliest Celtic societies, although not all Hallstatt people were Celts.

Iron was an important trade good for the Hallstatt people, as was salt. The latter was extremely important in preserving food, and control of the salt trade was highly lucrative. The ability to preserve food meant that a greater population could be supported, and, coupled with the ability to arm warriors with iron weapons, allowed a warlike people to field large and formidable forces.

The trade in iron and salt – and other goods besides – allowed the Celtic people of the Hallstatt region to flourish

LEFT: The way that the dead are treated is often used as an identifier for a given culture. The Hallstatt culture moved from cremation and burial of ashes in an urn to burial of the whole body surrounded by grave goods.

and to move into new areas. Trade also carried ideas and cultural trends, preventing the more distant Celtic people from diverging too far from the cultural norms of their brethren.

The Hallstatt culture was developing just as the Greek Dark Age was ending, and movement of Celtic people continued to occur. A new influx of Celts into Spain took place around 600 BCE, and at the same time the Greek outpost of Massilia (Marseilles) was founded at the mouth of the River Rhone in what is now southern France. Massilia became a major trade centre, through which the western Celts could obtain goods from all across the Mediterranean world.

La Tène Culture

An insight into later Celtic culture was provided by finds at La Tène, an archaeological site in Switzerland dating from 500 BCE onwards. The La Tène culture seems to be more warlike than the Hallstatt culture, and this era coincides with several migrations and invasions. Looking at the broad strokes of history, it is possible to infer that the Celts made several large movements, and certainly there were large-scale migrations by various people. However, movement of population was a constant activity, with small groups looking for a better place to live. Others might be seeking to escape from enemies or perhaps a social situation that they found disagreeable.

This constant small-scale movement makes it difficult to determine facts such as

BELOW: **Excavations at Hallstatt have given many insights into early Celtic culture, but any given site can give only a snapshot of what life was like in that particular locality during the time of its occupation.**

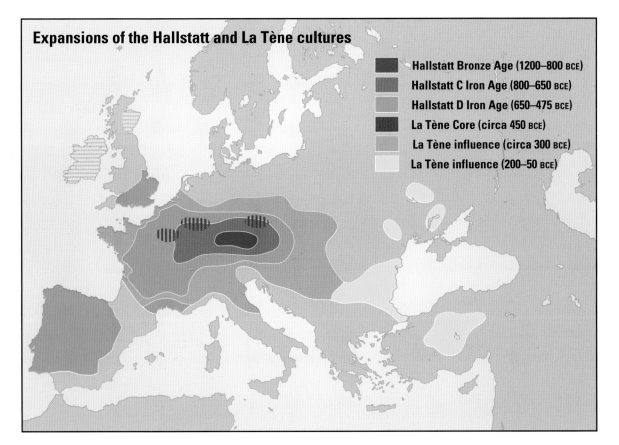

Expansions of the Hallstatt and La Tène cultures

- Hallstatt Bronze Age (1200–800 BCE)
- Hallstatt C Iron Age (800–650 BCE)
- Hallstatt D Iron Age (650–475 BCE)
- La Tène Core (circa 450 BCE)
- La Tène influence (circa 300 BCE)
- La Tène influence (200–50 BCE)

exactly when the British Isles were colonized by the Celts. It has been suggested that proto-Celtic people reached Britain anywhere between 2000 and 1200 BCE, and others came later. Some settled; others influenced proto-Celtic society through trade but did not remain to live in the British Isles. Ultimately, the British Isles became a Celtic region either through direct settlement or by 'Celtization' or a combination of both. The same is true of other regions in Europe, which were generally more accessible and thus even more thoroughly influenced.

As previously noted, the first crossing of the Alps by a Celtic tribe took place in 400 BCE or so. This brought the Celtic people to the notice of Roman scholars, from whose records much of what we know about the Celts is derived. The expedition was highly successful in that the Celts were able to establish themselves in Northern Italy where they remained a strong influence for many years.

However, long before Roman scholars began to write what

ABOVE: Although archaeological evidence seems to indicate clear cultural phases, the supplanting of the Hallstatt culture by the later La Tène culture, and its subsequent spread, was a gradual process in most areas and was also subject to outside influences.

ABOVE: **The Celtic Hypogeum at Cividale del Friuli in northern Italy was apparently constructed by enlarging a natural cavity. Its purpose remains unknown, though it has been suggested that it may have been intended as a burial site.**

they knew (and what they conjectured) about these newcomer barbarians, the Celts were well established as an Iron Age culture with distinct characteristics, and it was this culture that formed the basis of much of European society.

Greece and South-Eastern Europe

The Celtic people came into contact with Greek civilization as they moved southwards into the Balkans and also by way of trade ports such as Massilia. This city was founded by Greeks from Phocaea in Anatolia, on land given to them by the local rulers, and grew rapidly in size and importance. After Phocaea was overrun by the Persian Empire, many of its citizens relocated to colonies such as Massilia, which became large enough to create satellite settlements of its own.

The surrounding Celts were a major source of goods and a lucrative market for trade passing through Massilia. With few other trade ports in Western Europe, overland trade was carried on through the Celtic lands in order to reach more distant partners. This contributed to the prosperity of the local Celtic tribes, and also allowed cultural influences to pass both ways between Greeks and Celts.

Greek sources claim that the Celts learned about the rule of law and the skills necessary to carry out successful agriculture via trade with the Greeks, although it is likely that the Celts already had a good grasp of both before the Greeks arrived. After the rise of Rome, Massilia remained an important trade link between Gaul and Italy (and the rest of the Roman world).

It is possible that Greek influences beginning around 600 BCE were partly responsible for the evolution in Celtic society that becomes apparent when comparing the Hallstatt and La Tène cultures. These influences came in part via Massilia and the Rhone valley, but were also produced by direct contact with the Greek heartlands.

Contact with the Greeks had probably been going on, at least to a minor extent, for many years before the first incidences are recorded in history. The Hallstatt culture was maturing at the same time that the Greeks were emerging from their dark age, and it seems likely that Celtic traders or migrating groups would have wandered into the Balkans and come into contact with the Greeks at some point.

From around 400 BCE onwards, about the same time as some tribes were pushing south across the Alps into Italy, Celtic groups began to settle Danube valley and gradually move south-eastwards. In 335 BCE, Celtic envoys negotiated a treaty with Alexander the Great, sending warriors to assist in

BELOW: **Many Celtic coins show Greek influences in the images they display. Later coinage often features more abstract versions of the same concepts, perhaps indicating lessening Greek influence and the emergence of quintessentially Celtic art.**

OPPOSITE: **The idea that Celts liked to fight naked is open to some question. It may be that in art, such as this sarcophagus, nakedness is used to portray the Galatians and other Celts as barbarians. It is possible that it was conventional to portray the Celts this way, and the sculptor was simply following fashion.**

his wars. Some of the latter ended up in Italia, fighting against the Etruscans, while others served as mercenaries elsewhere.

After the death of Alexander in 323 BCE, the fragmentation of his empire permitted the Celts to push into the Balkans and seize territory there. The Celtic invasion of Greece began in 279 BCE. Various reasons have been put forward for it, ranging from simple opportunism to population pressure or a need to find productive lands during a famine. After successes against Macedonian forces, this 'great expedition' was repulsed at the pass of Thermopylae by a force from several Greek cities.

After eventually managing to outflank the Greek army at Thermopylae, the Celts attacked Delphi but were defeated, with rival groups within the Celtic force turning on one another in the aftermath. Further Greek attacks drove the Celts out of Greece, but opinions are divided among historians as to whether or not this constitutes abject defeat. True, the Celts were forced to retreat but it has been contended that their aim was never conquest, only plunder. The survivors of the great expedition did manage to carry off sufficient loot to make the enterprise worthwhile, which might have been the aim all along.

'GALATIAN WARRIORS WERE HIGHLY REGARDED AND WERE HIRED AS MERCENARIES.'

Some of the Celts involved in the Greek adventure settled in Thrace, in modern-day Bulgaria and Turkey. Some went further, taking service with Nicomedes I of Bithynia for which they were granted lands in Anatolia (in modern-day Turkey). Founded in 275 BCE, this Celtic enclave became known as Galatia. The Galatians were more heavily influenced by Greek culture than their European brethren, and have at times been referred to as Gallo-Graeci, which translates roughly as 'Gauls living among Greeks'.

Galatia's Celtic population was swelled by the arrival of related tribespeople from Europe, and the Celts were influential in the affairs of the region for many years. Galatian warriors were highly regarded and were hired as mercenaries (sometimes by both sides in a conflict) even when their tribes were not formally involved in a conflict.

Galatia lost its independence in 189 BCE when it was
conquered by Rome, and thereafter was a province of the Empire
except when the kingdom of Pontus dominated the region. The
Galatians took the side of Rome in the ensuing Mithridatic Wars
and although tribal rule was restored in 64 BCE, Galatia became
highly Romanized and was no longer culturally Celtic.

Iberia and the West

The proto-Celtic people spread westwards through Europe, eventually reaching the Iberian Peninsula. It is possible that the first arrivals were as early as 1300 BCE, with a second large-scale influx around 600 BCE. These Celts brought with them the Hallstatt culture, and found a variety of people already dwelling there.

A Phoenician outpost had been present in Iberia at Gades (modern Cadiz) from as early as 1100 BCE, serving as a trade port like others around the Mediterranean. The Phoenicians were joined around 600 BCE by Greeks and settlers from Carthage, who built the port of Carthago Nova (modern Cartagena).

These cultures were mainly influential in southern Iberia, along the Mediterranean coast, whereas the Celts entered over the Pyrenees and pushed into the peninsula from the north-east. Classical writings describe a period of conflict between the new arrivals and those already dwelling in Iberia, although it seems that the writers had little concrete information and were recording what was mainly conjecture and rumour.

Eventually, the Celts became part of the Iberian population, intermarrying and creating a mingled culture based around hill-

BELOW: The 'Bulls of Guisando' are four granite statues possibly dating from around 200–100 BCE. They, and others like them, are examples of Celtiberian art that may have been created by the Vettones tribal confederation.

forts. The society of these 'Celtiberians' gradually evolved from a tribal to a city-based culture, and was influenced by both Rome and Carthage. During the Punic Wars between Carthage and Rome, Celtiberian forces formed part of the Carthaginian army that advanced through the Alps into Italy, and after the defeat of Carthage Celtiberia fell increasingly under Roman influence.

This influence was, however, a two-way street. The two-edged sword used by Roman forces was sometimes known as the 'Spanish sword' (Gladius Hispaniensis), having been invented in Iberia and adopted as a sidearm by Roman troops. It replaced an earlier Greek-style weapon that dated from the original Greek style of warfare practiced – often without much success – by earlier Roman forces.

Hispania, as the Romans called the region, was increasingly Romanized as time passed, and was later subject to invasion by migrating Germanic tribes and – later still – the Moors. This

ABOVE: **This Celtic village in Spain used the same round house concept as elsewhere, but since stone was readily available locally it was used as a building material rather than the more common wattle-and-daub method of constructing walls.**

created a series of conflicts and upheavals that overlaid the Celtiberian culture with other customs and values. Elements of the original culture survived, but overall the region lost its Celtic flavour and eventually created a cultural identity of its own.

Gaul and Northern Europe

Gaul (modern-day France) was easily accessible to the migrating proto-Celts; more so than Italy or Iberia, which required crossing mountain ranges to enter. The proto-Celts were able to move into the region over time, bringing with them the Hallstatt culture and its predecessors. By around 500 BCE, most of Gaul had a recognizably Hallstatt-like culture, but this was apparently displaced quite quickly by the more militaristic La Tène culture from that time onwards.

The rise of the La Tène culture may indicate a period of greater conflict, but may also be simply due to the influence of neighbouring tribes. As one group adopted a more militaristic outlook, so others would tend to do likewise out of self-preservation. The best defence against a nearby society with well-equipped warriors who were willing to come and take what they wanted – and felt entitled to do so – was to have the same sort of warriors available.

There may have been an additional, economic impetus to this evolution. There was work to be had for warriors protecting trade expeditions coming out of Massilia, or as mercenaries hired to fight in other parts of the Mediterranean world. Fighting men could generate wealth for their tribe, paying for their status in a direct manner.

Whatever the reasons, Celtic culture in what would become known as Gaul became increasingly martial in the years before contact with Rome. It was the Romans who applied the label 'Gauls' to the barbarian warriors who came over the Alps to eventually plunder the Eternal City, and this label came to apply to anyone who looked, talked and fought like those people.

Although the term 'Gauls' was a generalization applying to Celtic people in general, the name 'Gaul' (or Gallia) was applied to the Celtic homelands in what is today France and the surrounding area. Depending on context, Gauls could be people

LEFT: This statue of a Gallic warrior and his horse is one of four decorating the Pont d'Iena. The possession of a horse was a status symbol even among those who fought on foot.

from Gallia, or barbarians who resembled them but hailed from other regions. This can be confusing to readers of Roman writings.

Celtic dominance in Gaul was first challenged by Rome in 125 BCE, leading to the annexation of the surrounding area. It was several decades later that the rest of Gaul was invaded and conquered, leading to several hundred years of Roman rule that did not succeed in demolishing the Celtic culture of the region. Romano-Gallic culture formed the basis for the early feudal kingdoms of Western Europe, and ultimately influenced the development of Western civilization.

The British Isles

Evidence has been found that the British Isles were inhabited as much as 800,000 years ago, at a time when the climate was considerably warmer. These people were not modern humans, and in any case would have been driven south or exterminated by the last glacial period, which began around 100,000 years ago. For tens of thousands of years the British Isles were covered in ice, which retreated rapidly after the last glacial maximum around 20,000 years ago.

OPPOSITE: The quintessentially 'Roman' weapon was the Gladius Hispaniensis ('Spanish Sword'). It was derived from traditional weapons encountered in the hands of Celtiberian warriors, and constructed in essentially the same way.

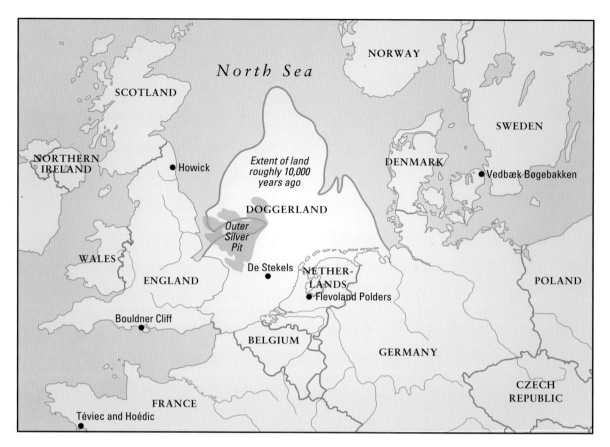

ABOVE: **Humans could easily move into what would become the British Isles until the submergence of Doggerland about 6000–8000 BCE. Even after this, the narrow sea was not a major barrier to trading expeditions and small-scale population migration.**

The retreat of the glaciers was accompanied by a rise in sea levels that inundated low-lying areas such as Doggerland (now part of the North Sea bed) and caused what would become the British Isles to become first a peninsula and then an island group.

It is likely that humans crossed into what would become the British Isles over a land bridge as the glaciers retreated at the end of the last Ice Age. Exactly when the region was cut off from Europe is still open to debate, but it is likely that some time between 8000 and 6000 BCE access was impeded by at least a narrow expanse of sea.

By this time there was already a substantial population in the area. Evidence has been found of human habitation in Ireland dating from 7000–8000 BCE, and the population was substantial by 1000 BCE. Some of these people may have been proto-Celts; others probably belonged to other groups or dated from a period before the proto-Celts and other genetic/ethnic groups had become recognizable.

It is likely that Celtic or proto-Celtic people migrated fairly slowly into the British Isles. Many of the early arrivals were traders who went home again once their business was concluded, but gradually the numbers of Celts in Britain increased and their culture became dominant.

Significant numbers of Celts arrived in Britain in the period 500 to 100 BCE, in some cases propelled by a desire to escape Roman conquest of their homelands. However, their ancestors had probably been migrating into the British Isles for a 1000 or perhaps 1500 years previously. The new arrivals joined a population that had many genetic and cultural similarities, and gradually a Celtic society in Britain emerged.

This society was characterized by similar martial trappings as the La Tène culture of the Continent; warriors provided protection and fighting prowess was often a requirement of rulership. Fortified settlements were common. Some of these were very small, being little more than a few houses or even a single fortified dwelling for an extended family. Quite elaborate hill-forts were also constructed, and while it is possible that this was done just out of habit, it seems unlikely.

'IT IS LIKELY THAT CELTIC OR PROTO-CELTIC PEOPLE MIGRATED FAIRLY SLOWLY INTO THE BRITISH ISLES.'

LEFT: Celtic constructions can be found throughout the British Isles. Naturally defensible places were often enhanced with simple stone and earth fortifications to create a well-protected settlement, suggesting that conflict was not uncommon.

Fortification work, however basic, requires a very significant investment in terms of time and effort, and is not likely to have been undertaken just for the sake of it. Thus it seems likely that the situation in Britain was much the same as elsewhere – fortified settlements were required to provide protection from natural hazards and human enemies. Perhaps they served a deterrent role, or were status symbols for the builders – those that could afford the time away from subsistence work to build fortifications were clearly well-off. A combination of all these factors is likely.

The Celtic people of the British Isles developed different identities over time. Those in Ireland probably arrived by way of a land bridge from Scotland, and gradually spread across the island. As sea levels rose and access from the rest of Britain became more difficult, the Irish Celts went their own way. Settlements were typically a small fortified stead, often on a hilltop. Known as rath, these steads have given their name to a great many places in Ireland.

Ireland lay beyond the reach of the Roman Empire but was eventually settled by Vikings, who lived alongside the Celts and

BELOW: **An Iron Age dwelling in Ballina, County Mayo, Ireland. It can be difficult at times to determine whether a given settlement was definitively Celtic or belonged to some other Iron Age culture that might be influenced by the Celtic way of life.**

warred with them at times. On other occasions they became involved in the complex wars and interactions of various Celtic groups. With the Viking settlement came the rise of several large and powerful towns; Celtic society was more dispersed and based around family and tribal associations.

The Celts of Wales and Scotland also remained at least partly outside the power of Rome. Although Wales was within the part of Britain conquered by Roman forces, it was less tightly controlled than more central areas and was heavily Romanized than what would later become England. Celtic culture survived more intact there than elsewhere.

The region that is now Scotland successfully resisted Roman incursions despite repeated attempts to bring it within the control of the Empire. Tribes along the border interacted with Roman Britain and were influenced by Roman values, while those farther north were less affected. The rest of Britain, on the other hand, was heavily Romanized after the conquest, leading to the creation of a Romano-British society in which Celtic influences were diminished in importance.

ABOVE: Celtic ringforts of varying sizes abound in Wales. The fortifications might be of earth or stone, and may also include a palisade of stakes. The Welsh term for such a fortified settlement is rath.

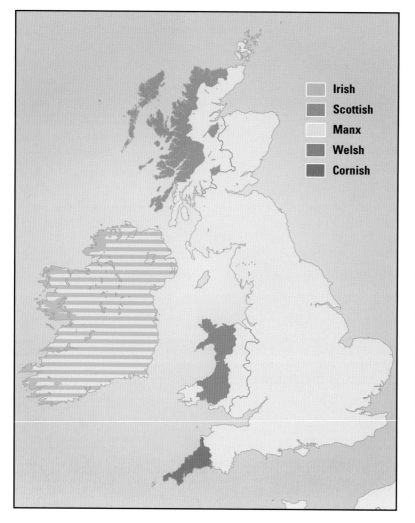

Irish
Scottish
Manx
Welsh
Cornish

By 800 BCE, the proto-Celtic people were developing into what we now recognize as a fully Celtic society. Before this, proto-Celts exhibited a number of traits that would later be associated with Celtic culture, which had developed as part of a transition going back perhaps as far as 3500 BCE. It is generally thought that the proto-Celts originated in Eastern Europe around this time and gradually spread across northern Europe as well as southwards into northern Greece and eventually across the Alps into Italy.

Celtic Language

These people were all connected by a common

ABOVE: **Numerous branches of the Celtic language family emerged over time, diverging from their common roots to create related but distinct languages. Many still exist today, and in some cases are deliberately preserved by education programmes.**

language family, now generally referred to as Old Celtic. This was derived from the same Indo-European language group as the Germanic tongues and also Italic, the precursor of Latin. Many customs and social structures were also similar, creating a widespread culture group with some local variations. The similarities between Celtic groups at opposite ends of Europe might have been startling to a traveller of 800 BCE or so, but from today's viewpoint it is possible to see the reasons for this near-homogeneity, as the development of Celtic and proto-Celtic society can be traced back through earlier European cultures.

Most of the languages spoken in Europe come from a common origin, which developed between 3000 and 2000 BCE. From this original tongue came the Celto-Italic group of languages, one of which developed into Latin and then into the modern language group known as the Romance languages.

Two main Celtic language groups, known as Goidelic and Brythonic, developed from the original, and these gradually evolved into later tongues such as Gaelic. Many of the Celtic languages, especially those of the Continent such are Gaulish, are extinct although vestiges survive in place names and words adopted by other languages. Some, such as Breton, Welsh, Irish and Scottish Gaelic, are still spoken by significant numbers of native or secondary speakers in their home regions, and by a smaller displaced population in the Americas.

The Brythonic languages were spoken by a group now referred to as the p-Celts. Their languages were the forerunners of Welsh, Cornish and Breton, and were brought to the British Isles later than the Goidelic tongues, probably as a result of immigration from the Continent. The main forerunner of these is British, the main Celtic language of mainland Britain around 100 BCE.

The Goidels, or q-Celts, spoke an earlier language that was brought into the British Isles with immigrants and traders around 2000–1200 BCE. Goidelic was predominant in Ireland and gradually became the main Celtic language of what is now Scotland. Irish Gaelic (usually just called Irish) and Scottish Gaelic continued to evolve along divergent paths after the end of the main Celtic era, and were influenced by other languages such as Norse.

Although there were differences between the Celtic languages, common roots made it likely that any given group of Celts could communicate reasonably well with any other. This commonality of language was more than merely a sharing of words; it was based on a similar way of thinking and on a common set of values and beliefs. To an outsider, one group of Celts would look and sound – and probably behave – much like another. To the Celts themselves, however, the differences were probably very apparent.

BELOW: Kilnasaggart Stone is one of the oldest known inscribed stones in Ireland. The inscriptions and early Christian burials nearby suggest that its origins are Christian, but the concept of inscribed stones probably predates Christianity in Ireland.

CELTIC SOCIETY

Although often depicted as raging barbarians, the Celts were anything but. They possessed excellent metalworking skills that enabled them to create high-quality weapons, but they also made ploughs and beautiful jewellery as well.

The Celts interacted meaningfully and mostly peaceably with other groups, trading with distant civilizations. They were able to bring needed items into a region where they were scarce and to export what could be easily made there to the benefit of others.

The Celtic social system worked well enough that it came to dominate most of Europe. Celtic society was built around a social order that provided stability, at least most of the time. This was necessary for prosperity, as stability created conditions under which economic activity could flourish.

Without a stable society, even basic economic activities such as farming and herding would be disrupted, resulting in a reduced ability to support the population. Although cattle raids

OPPOSITE: Although sometimes depicted as simple barbarians, the Celts were entirely capable of building large towns, which were tied together by a sophisticated trade network. This town in Galicia contained hundreds of dwellings, suggesting a population in the thousands.

ABOVE: **Celtic farmers were the bedrock of their society since nothing else could be achieved if there was insufficient food to go around. Increased productivity due to well-made tools freed other workers to engage in different kinds of economic activity.**

and violent disputes were not uncommon, the Celtic social order kept these within acceptable limits and prevented society from breaking down beyond the point where specialists could be supported. Thus the fact that decorative items and high-quality goods could be made at all is proof that Celtic society was – for the most part – stable and successful.

If farms and herds were constantly under attack, production of basic foodstuffs could be disrupted so badly that society might fall back to the level of individual subsistence. Supporting a ruling class, warriors, religious leaders and specialist workers such as metalsmiths required sufficient surplus food that those who produced it could afford to trade some of it away. The strong could take from the weak for a while, but robbing the farmers too often would result in a decline in production that would eventually send the armed bands into the fields or the forests to hunt and grow their own food.

Even assuming that the producing classes were well enough protected to be able to go about their business more or less unmolested, society also had to produce sufficient confidence in the value of items and services that people were willing to trade. A warrior elite could simply tell farmers that they were required to deliver a suitable amount of food – or face the consequences – but a society in which the farming classes had confidence in their warriors and felt that supporting them was valuable would function far more smoothly.

Since inter-tribal raiding and general low-level violence was not uncommon, the existence of skilled fighters who could provide effective protection had a real and obvious value. Warriors returning from a raid, or who had defeated an attack from rivals, were an obvious sign of strength that would reassure the producing classes, while those injured or killed in action were a reminder that the elite paid a price for their status. Under good conditions, the relationship between warriors and farmers was based upon mutual respect. Both groups could see the value of the other's activities and were willing to support them. A well-integrated society of this sort was far more harmonious than one in which an armed elite took what they wanted and crushed the opposition.

The Warband

Although Celtic society did not support a professional warrior class as such, many leaders surrounded themselves with a warband of men who were well equipped, skilled and reliable in battle. These men were the first choice when someone had to go to deal with a problem, and although they would not be professional soldiers they were likely to be quite experienced. When a larger force was mustered from the general populace of the tribe, the warband served as an ideal of how to conduct oneself in battle and led the lesser fighters by example even if they were not formally placed in charge of others.

BELOW: **Initially, even those that owned a horse dismounted to fight, but over time the practice of fighting mounted became more widespread. At the time of Caesar's Gallic Wars, many Gaulish tribes could muster an effective cavalry force.**

The warband was an informal group, based on mutual respect, fighting prowess and trust. Had Celtic society broken down, these were the men who could force others to obey them by threats or deeds of violence, but for the most part the warband remained simply part of the accepted social order. If some men were on first-call for dealing with raids and other troubles then they could not be expected to be as productive as those farmers who were able to stay on their land throughout the incident. In a well-integrated society everyone understood the part played by others – and more importantly they could see that they played it fairly.

The benefit of specialists was more obvious and tangible. A metalsmith could make tools that the farmer or craftsman would use, weapons for the warriors and decorative items that could be traded or used as symbols of wealth and status. As with the farmers and herders, craftsmen needed stability to be able to carry out their function, and disruption to their activities could easily be seen to be bad for society.

BELOW: Although agriculture was a primary source of food, hunting also helped support the tribe. The bow was used for hunting, though it was rarely taken to war, while broad-bladed spears were used for both purposes.

The Celtic social order provided this stability – to a greater
or lesser degree depending on how hard times were – and the
benefits were obvious to all. The upper echelon of society was
made up of leaders, tribal officials and skilled craftsmen as well
as religious figures, with the producing classes below them. The
stability provided by this accepted social order made it possible
to produce enough food to support the higher echelons of society,
and they in turn produced crafted goods that made the workers'
tasks easier, brought in wealth by trade and equipped those that
fought for the tribe.

The prosperity of Celtic society is evident in their love of
decoration. They made art objects and individuals wore jewellery,
including torcs and arm rings of bronze and gold, as well as
clothing that was more than merely functional. Bright colours
and complex weaving patterns are not necessary, but they are
both pleasing and indicative of status. Barbarians on the edge of
survival do not concern themselves with clothing that pleases
the eye or commands respect; they devote all their efforts to
staying alive. It requires a civilization to create things of beauty,
and the Celts created a great many of those.

The term 'civilization' is rarely, if ever, applied to the Celts,
and it is not always obvious why. The Ancient Greeks were
every bit as subdivided as the Celtic tribes, and were no more
capable in terms of metalworking and similar critical skills.
Perhaps it is the lack of written records, great works and fine
cities filled with statues of the celebrated and the notorious that

renders the Celts unworthy of the term 'civilization', or perhaps it is merely that they were the enemies of the civilizations revered in recent history.

Whatever the reason, it is not common to refer to a Celtic civilization, but their society has all the hallmarks of one. Stability, trade, the rule of law and workable social customs, art and complex tools; they had everything necessary to be regarded as a true civilization. Perhaps the deciding factor is that what remains of the Celts tends to be lonely standing stones covered in strange designs, found in wild places. This creates an image of mystic barbarians that has misled generations, whereas great cities filled with monuments might have created a different image.

The Tribe, the Sept and the Family

Celtic society can be thought of in terms of a series of layers, each of which can be considered to be much like an increasingly extended family. The largest of these 'families' was the tribe. Of course, not everyone in a tribe was related to one another, but the tribe had a number of connotations. The tribal leaders and important figures had authority over the tribal members that was more familial than the formal legal authority of today's government officials or the divinely inspired kings of the middle ages.

'LAND WAS THE PROPERTY OF THE TRIBE AS A WHOLE, ALTHOUGH IT COULD BE OWNED BY INDIVIDUALS.'

Land was the property of the tribe as a whole, although it could be owned by individuals, and the same custom applied to cattle. This apparent contradiction meant that an individual could count land among his property but it could not be sold or traded. In this way an individual could not deprive the tribe of his land if he were convinced or coerced into selling it, and while he could sell or trade his cattle he required the permission of the tribe. This concept of common ownership died out in much of Europe as other social systems overlaid Celtic traditions, although it did persist in Highland Scotland for many generations.

The implications of this for the ruling class are complex. Tribal leaders could decide what was to be done with the tribe's property, but this was not quite the same as being the owner

of that property. A tribal leader who thought he could simply dictate to his people would likely cause outrage and might have quite a short career, so leaders had to rule by consent, if not necessarily consensus.

Working the Land

For those who used the land, whether they owned it or not, working it was a communal activity in which everyone played a part. Ploughing, planting and harvesting were large-scale activities that could be carried out more efficiently by a large number of people working together than would be possible with many small farms worked separately to the best of their owners' abilities.

This shared ownership of land and the cooperative working of it represented a major investment in the tribe by its members. The efforts of individuals directly contributed to the prosperity and success of the tribe, and the wellbeing of the tribe as a whole was a direct influence on the living standards of its members. This fostered respect for the other members of the tribe rather than competition against them – but only if tribe members had

ABOVE: **The chieftain's hall was a place of hospitality rather than grandeur, and the actions of the people within the hall were more important than the building itself. Visitors would take greater note of a host's personality than the architecture of his home.**

RIGHT: **It is probable that the ancient Celts invented a simple mechanical reaping machine, which severed the ears from corn and gathered them as it was pushed along. This technology fell into disuse after the 'Celtic Era' and was not rediscovered for over a thousand years.**

confidence that others were playing fair and pulling their weight.

Someone who did not meet the expected standards of effort, or who was incompetent, would be badly thought of by his peers. There were undoubtedly some who preferred to get as easy a ride as they could from the efforts of others, but being seen to put in a fair day's work and perhaps to outperform one's peers was a way to win respect.

There are numerous traditional games or sports that are still played in some areas, and which almost certainly originated as a contest between workmates. It is easy to see the origins of simple (but physically very demanding) games such as throwing a barrel or other heavy object over an obstacle, or getting a hay bale from one point to another. It is not usually possible to say if any given traditional sport is of Celtic origin, but it is the nature of men to invent contests using whatever is to hand so some variant of these games will likely have been played.

Most traditional sports of this kind are based on strength, endurance and skill or perhaps technique. In many cases they are a direct 'I can do it better than you' challenge to perform an extreme version of something the workers do for a living. As well as providing entertainment, these contests also helped establish the social order, with those whose power or proficiency made them stand out being admired and respected. This was important to the individual Celt, who hoped that by a combination of his appearance, his prowess and some judicious boasting to be well regarded by his fellow tribe members.

The tribe was the largest political grouping that the Celts maintained, acting in some ways as a sort of miniature nation and at other times as a guide as to who was 'us' and who was 'them'. The tribe's relations with other tribes and outside groups such as city-state trade ports or political entities like the emerging Roman Republic would change over time, and there might be disputes within a tribe as well, but overall the tribe served to delineate who an individual Celt felt obligations of kinship and shared effort towards.

Septs

Within a tribe there were subdivisions called septs, some of which had an almost entirely separate identity and very different customs from other septs. Septs were more or less independent of one another, although the septs of a tribe were bound by ties of kinship and loyalty to the tribe as a whole. It is generally easier for a person (of any era) to identify with a relatively small and close group; ties to a regiment are in general stronger than those to the army as a whole, and people usually identify more strongly with their home city, state or region than with their country.

BELOW: **This image of a Celtic village is based on the excavated site at Chysauster in Cornwall. This particular style of settlement was common only in the Channel Isles and Cornwall. Each dwelling had a walled yard and outbuildings opening off a walled courtyard.**

The situation was the same with septs and tribes; individual Celts had more interactions with, and closer personal loyalty to, their sept than to their tribe, and closer still ties with their clan or family. The Celtic concept of family was slightly different to that commonly accepted today. It can be described as a closely associated group of people who lived and worked together, of whom some were related by blood or marriage to at least some of the others.

Many Celts lived in small extended-family groups, working a farm or stead as a social and economic unit. A community of this sort would have a social hierarchy that was repeated on a larger scale throughout the immediate local areas, the sept and the tribe. The king of a tribe was in many ways just a grander version of the head of a family household, and actually held authority in much the same way.

There was no concept of divine or hereditary right to rule among the Celts. Kings and chieftains were elected by a combination of popular acclaim and general acceptance of a satisfactory situation. There were families that produced many kings and other important officials, but each was elected and maintained his (or her) power only through the continued approval of the tribe.

Upheaval was in no-one's interest, of course, so removing a chieftain was unusual. A chieftain did not have to curry favour and try to please the voters all of the time, but he did have to be mindful that if confidence was lost he would be replaced by someone who might do better. An unpopular chieftain

BELOW: Like many images of Celtic society, this depiction of the tribal king at a banquet probably reflects the expectations of the time it was created rather than historical reality. The general impression is more medieval rather than Celtic.

might retain power for lack of a suitable replacement or because he was able to convince the tribe that the present situation was better than the alternatives – or perhaps through fear and intimidation – but kings and chieftains ruled by consent and had to remain aware of it if they wanted to keep their positions.

Kings and chieftains were usually, but not always, men. A woman could be elected to high office, and some tribes were ruled by women for extended periods. This absolutely baffled some outsiders. Certain Roman writers were happy enough to record that beyond the known lands around their borders were tribes of vulture-headed men, but they considered tales of barbarians ruled by women to be a bit far-fetched.

ABOVE: **A Gallic chieftain armed with spear, shield and sword. He wears a fair amount of personal decoration such as an arm ring, partly to show how rich and important he is and partly because the Celts loved beautiful things for their own sake.**

The chieftains and kings of the Celts were not absolute rulers as later kings would be. Indeed, their role was to some extent that of an appointed executive officer, who was given the authority to make some decisions but was mostly charged with how a task was to be accomplished rather than what was to be done. Chieftains did not make laws nor could they – officially at least – dictate what the tribe was going to do. It is likely that some charismatic chieftains did exactly that and were willingly followed, but officially their role was to implement the overall will of the tribe.

That could at times be a problem, as a consensus might not be achieved or some parts of a tribe might have very different needs to others. A charismatic chieftain, in whom the people believed, could reconcile differences and guide his (or her) tribe while a less secure leader or a more fragmented tribe might be unable to act due to an excess of democracy at a critical time.

The Celtic Social Order

The social hierarchy in Celtic society was somewhat fluid. It was entirely possible for an individual to rise or fall in status through hard work or ill fortune. Since the tribal leaders were elected, it might seem that anyone could emerge from the masses to become a king, but the reality was somewhat more complex. In any given tribe there would be certain families that were held in high regard, usually due to a combination of wealth and past deeds.

Leaders would normally come from among these families, with individuals from outside this group having far less chance of being taken seriously as a candidate for high office. In many ways this group of established leader-candidates equated to a noble class, and of course rich and/or well-regarded people would wield a great deal of unofficial influence.

'THE ROMANS PAINTED THE DRUIDS AS VILLAINS WHO ENGAGED IN DARK AND BLOODY RITUALS.'

However, the top echelons of Celtic society, at least in terms of formal authority, were determined by an individual's function in the tribe.

As already noted, kings and chieftains ranked highest, followed by a professional class made up of druids and bards. The latter were the custodians of history and lore, using poetry and songs to remember and pass on tales of previous events. Like some other cultures, notably the Norse, the Celts preferred to trust their cultural memories to a professional caste of poets rather than commit them to writing. Bards not only recalled the past; they commemorated the present in new songs and poems, composing new material to record or venerate noteworthy deeds and events. Bards trained for many years and were highly valued in Celtic society, although the word 'bard' later came to have a derogatory meaning before returning to a different but more positive connotation in recent history.

Power of the Druids

The other professional group, the druids, wielded a great deal of power in Celtic society – sometimes more so than chieftains or kings. Much of what is 'known' today about druids is pure invention. The Romans painted the druids as villains who engaged in dark and bloody rituals, ruling their people through mystical fear or grim magic. Since the druids were more or less expunged by the Romans, this propaganda outlived the reality.

Similarly, the revival of interest in druidism from the eighteenth century onwards was largely based on an idealized guess at what druids might have been like, or even just wishful thinking. Although many of the ideas put forward at this time have entered into popular belief, modern scholarship has shown most of this 'knowledge' to be incorrect or, sometimes, simply made up.

The druids were a complex group. They were religious figures but also acted as doctors and lawyers. They could mediate disputes and had authority that crossed tribal boundaries. This gave them the ability to settle conflicts between tribes if necessary, and in many matters their word carried greater weight than that of a chieftain. This came at the price of extremely long training – perhaps as much as two decades.

BELOW: **The popular image of druids as mystical figures receiving veneration and submission even from proud warriors is at least part invention. Druids were, however, wielders of great social power and influence – whatever their magical capabilities might have been.**

RIGHT: The family home was the heart of the Celtic tribe. A typical family worked the land and had a few livestock, and provided one or more fighting men to the tribe in times of trouble.

Between the highly trained professional class and the bulk of the tribe were a collection of elected officials. These were the administrators of the tribe, and the chieftain can be considered to be simply the first and highest-ranked among them. Elected officials oversaw large-scale organization such as the redistribution of food to ensure that those who suffered a bad harvest did not starve or the construction of projects such as roads.

The main social group in a Celtic tribe was made up of economic producers. Tribesmen who owned some land and farmed it, or who fulfilled an equivalent function such as smiths, formed the backbone of a tribe's wealth and were its most influential members. This class of individual had a strong voice in the running of the tribe, and contributed most to its success. Those that did not hold land, or were employed by others rather than running their own business, had lesser status since they contributed less to the well-being of the tribe as a whole.

Celtic Underclass

The lowest social class in Celtic society were those that were not free. These were not slaves in the usual sense – the Celts did not believe a person could be owned. They were, however, those who had a debt to the tribe and were not free until it was paid. This class included criminals who had been sentenced to work until they were considered to have paid their debt to society and also captives taken in war. The latter were not enslaved but would be held (and put to work to earn their keep) until their family or tribe paid a ransom. They could also be killed out of hand if they proved troublesome.

Capturing enemies for ransom was a well-established custom, and served a number of purposes. Obviously it enriched those who received the ransom but it also meant that there was a real financial incentive to spare a defeated enemy. This meant that he would eventually return home and resume working his fields or craft, rather than depriving the tribe of an economically useful individual.

The practice of ransom reduced the severity of warfare, helping to keep inter-tribal conflicts within acceptable limits. A protracted war, with battles to the death, would wear down all participants whereas a more limited conflict was unlikely to cripple either side. In the long term this was beneficial to Celtic society as a whole.

Had there existed a professional military class this might not have been so, but the Celts did not maintain a standing army or even a body of professional warriors. In time of war, the farmer-crafter class provided most of the fighting men, with some coming from the lower hired-worker class. Among these, there would be some elite warriors who had a great deal of experience or who were sufficiently wealthy to be able to spare time for training.

It might be possible for a skilled fighter to live well on the

'IN TIME OF WAR, THE FARMER-CRAFTER CLASS PROVIDED MOST OF THE FIGHTING MEN.'

ABOVE: Although depicted as a hunter, this Gaulish tribesman seems to be armed for war. His spear could be used in hunting, but it hardly seems appropriate to the prey he has bagged. Nor does one need a shield for protection when hunting fowl.

proceeds of ransom, and some members of society might well be semi-professional warriors. However, the bulk of casualties in any war were landed or skilled freemen whose economic value to the tribe was considerable. Even leaving aside considerations of the personal impact of a lost brother, son or father, the death of a tribesman affected everyone, so if he could be ransomed back then this was in the tribe's best interests.

Economy and Trade

The basis of any economy is the ability to feed the population. It is possible to import food by trade, but more commonly farming, herding, fishing and hunting are the bedrock of any society. Without sufficient food, Celtic society would have collapsed.

Fortunately for the Celts, they had some significant advantages in this area. The advent of iron tools allowed the creation of greatly improved ploughs that could cut through heavy soil. Earlier ploughs, typically made of wood, could only scrape a groove into the surface, and were useful mainly on fairly loose soil such as found in upland areas. The more advanced iron plough allowed heavier and more fertile lowland soils to be worked, and could turn the soil over rather than grooving it.

This enabled the Celts to grow more food than previous cultures, although ploughing was an arduous business requiring the cooperative efforts of several people as well as a team of oxen. The latter was a big investment, beyond the means of most individual farmers, but was achievable on a communal basis. Fields were long and narrow due to the difficulty of turning the team and the plough around, but since ploughing was a cooperative effort a team could work several farmers' land at the same time.

Salt was also important to food availability. It was useful as flavouring, but more importantly it allowed food to be preserved for the winter months or to be transported in trade. The Hallstatt region contained several salt mines, which was beneficial in terms of food availability and also trade in salt itself.

The Hallstatt region also had good access to tin, which was vital in bronze making, and this too was traded widely until the end of the Bronze Age. It is possible that the introduction of widespread iron use resulted from the Bronze Age Collapse and its associated reduction in the availability of copper, the other constituent of bronze. With the Celts' main sources of copper out of the picture for the time being, there was a need for a replacement and iron was the obvious choice.

Although harder to obtain from its ore than copper or tin, iron did not necessarily make superior tools or weapons than bronze. Early iron items were not notably more durable than those they replaced, although by the time copper was available again in sufficient quantities to resume bronze making, ironsmithing had improved to the point where there was no reason to return to bronze-working.

BELOW: The heavy ox-plough enabled Celtic farmers to work heavier soils and to get much more productivity out of their fields. Its invention triggered a rapid population expansion that enabled Celtic society to spread all across Europe.

Salt, tin and later on iron goods were all important exports for the Hallstatt Celts, who also benefited from a central location that allowed a trade network to grow. Trade links were created all across Europe, often making use of rivers to carry large cargoes cheaply. Coastal shipping and wagons operating on a basic but effective road network also carried trade all across Europe.

Celts of all regions were famed for their metalworking skills, and their decorative items – especially jewellery made from gold – were traded far and wide. Weapons were also valued, along with high-quality clothing that was often dyed in bright colours and eye-catching patterns.

These goods were traded for whatever the Celts needed, with sufficient surplus to buy luxuries. Greek wine was particularly popular; pottery amphorae used to transport and store wine have been found in large quantities at Celtic archaeological sites, and wine was buried with some Celts. Presumably this was to symbolize prosperity, or perhaps so that an important individual would have something nice to drink in the afterlife.

Direct barter of goods for goods was always possible, but coinage offered a more readily portable medium of exchange. The idea of coins probably came into Europe via Greece around 600 BCE, and was quickly adopted in most areas. Many Celtic tribes minted their own coins, using both gold and silver, and inscribed them according to local preferences.

Coinage was not initially a representative currency; a coin was worth the weight of gold or silver it contained, and was minted as a simple way of delineating a given amount of precious metal. Celtic coins, at least initially, were heavily influenced by Greek coinage and often carried inscriptions in Greek. Designs became more abstract over time, and more quintessentially Celtic than the original Greek-style images.

BELOW: **This bronze horse statue is rather primitive in its execution, and may have been a child's toy or an apprentice-piece. A metalsmith did not learn to make intricate jewellery or durable weapons overnight; he would create increasingly complex pieces until he mastered his craft.**

Gender Roles, Sexuality and Social Rituals

It has been observed about Celtic society that the men would engage in all manner of petty bickering and fights for the slightest of reasons, but once a Celt's wife got involved, things became deadly serious. This was not an uncommon situation in ancient societies as it reflected the nature of life in the era.

A tribe could stand to lose a certain proportion of its men to pointless fights and machismo-induced misadventure; indeed, it might actually be beneficial to weed out the incompetent, the clumsy and the most excessively belligerent members of the tribe. However, if a situation became sufficiently serious that the wellbeing of society were threatened then women would take notice.

Stupidity of various sorts could be brought to a rapid halt by the intervention of wives and mothers, and proud men were given an 'honourable out' if their stated intentions were curtailed by sharp words from the womenfolk. Conversely, if a conflict reached the point where the tribe's women became involved then it was obviously an extremely serious matter and the fighting-men would be expected to give their all in the hopes of victory.

Women were sometimes elected as tribal leaders, but it was rare for a woman to fight. Archaeologists have found female burials containing weapons, but this is not proof of the existence of female warriors. It is more likely that the weapons and war equipment found in these burials was indicative of social status, perhaps as a chief or leader, rather than suggesting the owner was a warrior.

However, although there is relatively little evidence either way, it does seem that Celtic society had softer gender-role boundaries than many other cultures of the same era. Women could own property and be powerful in their own right, acting as

ABOVE: **This coin from the La Tène era (around 450 BCE) shows a clear, if stylized, image. Later coinage featured increasingly abstract representations of the same themes as Greek influences diminished and a more 'Celtic' flavour emerged.**

ABOVE: **This image of a druidess contains all the popular elements; white robe, golden sickle and mistletoe, and there is even a stone henge in the background. The reality of druidism was probably quite different, though little evidence has survived.**

merchants and ambassadors between tribes. Women could also become druids, wielding spiritual authority and acting as doctors or lawyers in the same manner as a male druid.

This level of egalitarianism shocked many Roman writers, who came from a society where women had little personal freedom or power. The idea that women could lead a tribe – and that men would allow themselves to be subject to the commands of a woman – was sufficiently repugnant to the Romans that it was used as evidence of the Celts' barbarism and general strangeness.

Similarly, women enjoyed a great deal of sexual freedom in Celtic society compared with the Roman custom. A woman could openly have relations with whatever men she chose, and was not subject to the same sort of social judgement. In all probability, women (and men) in Celtic society were no more or less promiscuous than anyone else, but the lack of shame and the feeling that there was no need for secrecy seems to have puzzled Roman writers, among others.

Similarly, the Romans seem to have been puzzled by relations between men. Some writers recorded that although Celtic women were beautiful, their men seemed to prefer their own sex. This may or may not have been the case; it is quite possible that the Romans completely misinterpreted the relationships between Celtic men and assumed that they were lovers. However, there are enough accounts to suggest that homosexual relationships could exist openly. Indeed, the

Celts seem to have had a fairly open-minded attitude to sexual relations in general.

In a society with a relaxed attitude towards sexual relations, it is not surprising that society was accepting of children born outside of an established marriage. Where there was a relationship, the child was the joint responsibility of both parents and their families, but in all cases a child born to a member of the tribe was accepted by the tribe as legitimate.

Where there was not an established parental household, the child was raised by its mother if the father was a foreigner, excessively poor or otherwise unsuitable; or by the father if the mother was unable to look after her child. It was not uncommon for a child to be fostered by relatives or members of the same community until at least the early teens, usually later in the case of boys. A child with a single parent could thus be given a new home if this seemed appropriate, although undoubtedly there were numerous single-parent Celtic families.

Marriage and kinship were important factors in Celtic society, and other than a spiritual element in the form of solemn vows there was no real religious connotation. A marriage was more in the form of a contract between two people, which dealt with ownership of property and the rights of any offspring. This does not mean that a wedding was not a romantic occasion, nor that marriages were always simply pragmatic partnerships, but Celtic society regarded marriage as very much an agreement between people rather than a divine gift.

Marriage Bonds

The ancient Celts lived in an era when life could be hard, so a marriage that was purely for love might prove to be a disaster for all concerned. A good marriage created a partnership

BELOW: **Although druids oversaw the wedding ceremony and religious oaths were taken, marriage was very much an earthly matter to the Celts. Many couples undertook a fixed trial period called handfasting, after which they chose to separate or make a full marriage commitment.**

that was stronger and more resilient than the two individuals would be separately, enabling the family to survive tough times and prosper when things were good. Many marriages were arranged by the families involved, and there was a lot more to choosing a partner than physical attractiveness or personal compatibility.

Marriages involved property, status and kinship, and were thus of concern to relatives of both prospective partners. A marriage would build ties between families, which might or might not be beneficial. Status was very important in Celtic society, so relatives might try to prevent their relatives from marrying into a low-status family. There were other mechanisms to prevent this, too. A husband-to-be was required to present the bride's family with a bride-price, which might be more than he could afford if she were from a rich household.

We do not know what practices were followed in Continental Europe; much of the Celtic law we have comes from Ireland and Wales, where it survived to be adopted into the late body of law. However, cultural similarities are such that some version of Irish

BELOW: Reconstructed Celtic houses give an insight not only into how people lived but also their building and crafting techniques. Each house in this reconstructed village is based on a different design that has been found and studied by archaeologists.

and Welsh practice probably was used on the Continent.

Celtic law recognized several degrees of what might be termed 'marriage', in this case a rather loose term generally relating to sexual relations. The most well-respected and desirable unions were between people of equal status and property, and if one partner was richer then it was preferable for it to be the man. A marriage to someone who had no property and was supported entirely by the richer partner was only a little higher regarded than an agreement to live separately but have sex whenever it suited both partners, or a 'soldier's marriage' that was essentially a brief sexual liaison.

Seduction, rape and the union of insane people rank lower on the scale of desirability, but – oddly, perhaps, to the modern reader – they are on the list. This is largely because marriage was primarily about protecting the rights of offspring, so any way a child could be produced had to be accounted for. There was no concept of illegitimacy in Celtic society – children belonged to the tribe and were thus tribespeople like everyone else.

Celtic society permitted people to have more than one married partner. Usually it was men who had two or more wives, but a woman might have more than one husband if she chose. The first partner was senior and had full rights to be consulted in any agreement made by their husband (or, less commonly, wife), while additional wives had much less say in the affairs of the household. Indeed, while the first wife was essentially co-owner of everything the family had, additional wives received support only so long as the husband insisted upon it – the first wife had no obligations towards them.

ABOVE: Much of Celtic marriage law was about protecting and providing for any children that might be produced. If the parents separated or one of them was killed in war, the tribe had a responsibility to ensure the welfare of their offspring.

ABOVE: **The family unit was essential to Celtic society. A married couple were often more of an asset to the tribe than two single people, so long as they formed an effective team whose skills and strengths complemented one another.**

Before marrying, a couple could try out the idea through the practice of handfasting. This was somewhere between a modern engagement and a true marriage, and lasted for a year and a day. At the end of that time, the couple could go their separate ways with no obligations regarding property, or could decide to formalize their marriage. Handfastings usually took place at religious festivals or tribal gatherings (often both occurred at the same time) and thus generally were associated with religiously or socially significant times of year.

A handfasting that did not end in marriage was the end of the matter; the former couple separated and were not considered to have ever been married. They might try again in the future, or find a new partner, and eventually become married. This was a more complex situation if it ended, because marriage – unlike handfasting or sexual liaisons outside marriage – affected property ownership.

Divorce carried no social stigma as such, it was simply the end of a contract that had previously existed. However, it had to be settled legally and fairly. Thus while a marriage could be dissolved simply because one or both partners no longer wanted to be in that marriage, the reason for the divorce was extremely important. If one party (or both) simply decided to end it, property was divided as fairly as possible. Each got back whatever they had brought into the marriage and a share of anything gained since the day of their wedding.

However, if a man or woman gave their partner grounds for divorce then the wronged party got much more. In many cases, the wronged party was entitled to the entire family estate, with the perpetrator of the offence left to cope as best they could. Grounds for divorce varied from place to place but could include betraying a man to his enemies, hitting a wife hard enough to leave a mark, dishonouring one another by words or deeds – or having bad breath.

A woman could also divorce her husband if he failed in his duty to provide adequately for the family, or failed to fulfil his sexual obligations to her for reasons such as homosexuality, impotence or a preference for another woman. Adultery and various forms of abuse were also considered grounds for divorce.

In other areas, there were well-established social customs, most notably the laws of hospitality. The Celts were, on the whole, a hospitable people who felt that guests needed to be made welcome and well looked after, but this was a two-way street. A guest could expect to be treated as well as the host could afford in terms of food, drink and a place to sleep, but in return he was expected to be respectful towards the host and his family, and most especially not to cause trouble or quarrel with the host's household.

Performance of songs or poems, or the telling of tales, was an important part of hospitality and of social

BELOW: The sharing of songs and tales was an important part of Celtic society, and professional bards were usually made welcome wherever they went. In return, they would sing the praises of their host both in his hall and wherever else they travelled.

life in general. A guest was expected to reward his hosts with a song or tale, and at feasts or other gatherings it was common for performances to take place. Bards were professionals at this, of course, but others would also take their turn and could win admiration for their efforts.

Personal appearance was also of great importance to the Celts. They bathed and washed frequently, and are credited with having invented soap. Men were generally clean-shaven other than their impressive moustaches, and hair was dressed with lime to make it stand up. Mirrors of bronze were used by both sexes, and it was considered unacceptable to be dirty or wear damaged clothing in public.

BELOW: **Celtic smiths produced finely decorated bronze mirrors. In a society that placed great importance on personal appearance they were highly valued both as useful items and for their craftsmanship.**

Celtic Law

Much of what we know about Celtic law comes from Ireland, where the Brehon Law of the pre-Christian Celts survived to be codified and written down as the basis of common law in the Christian period. Much of the body of law covered matters such as social etiquette, obligations to the tribe and to individuals, and the rules governing hospitality.

A key component in Celtic law was the rank or 'worth' of an individual, as determined by his or her social status and the amount of property he owned. This was termed the honour-price of that individual, and was in turn used to determine the honour-price of members of his close household. Thus a rich man's son might not yet own his father's estate, but his honour-price was based upon its worth.

It was assumed that the word of a high-status person was worth more than that of a common tribesman, and that an offence against a high-ranking person should carry a more serious penalty. This seems unfair to today's thinking, but in a society where social mobility was common it may have seemed more acceptable since anyone could aspire to become

LEFT: Much of what we know about Celtic law comes to us from Irish Brehon Law. This was administered by individuals normally referred to as judges, but whose role might better be described as 'scholars of law'.

a high-status person. The concept also makes sense in terms of value to the tribe. A druid or tribal official was worth more to his tribe than a farm labourer, so harming a high official harmed the tribe more.

Killing or harming someone carried a penalty in the form of a fine based either on a flat standard for all free members of the tribe or on the victim's honour-price. There were also numerous laws against sexual assault and rape, which again required the payment of a fine to compensate the victim. Interestingly, killing someone and trying to conceal the deed was considered more reprehensible than open slaying, and carried a much higher price. Similarly, the giving of an injury that the victim might survive but would not recover fully from was subject to a higher fine than simply killing them.

In this case a medical opinion would be sought nine days after the injury was inflicted, and if the physician thought that the victim would not fully recover, the fine was payable. If the victim was thought likely to recover, or at least survive, then the perpetrator was financially responsible for his medical

ABOVE: **This Irish carving of two chieftains apparently depicts them coming to an agreement. A contract or agreement was an important matter, and no-one was allowed to enter into a deal with a value greater than his own honour-price.**

treatment and upkeep for the duration of the injury.

The paying of the fine was the end of the matter, but if it were not paid then the family of the victim were free to exact whatever vengeance they pleased. This would likely take the form of finding and killing the perpetrator. If he fled, his family were responsible for his fine and were expected to either pay it or pursue him on behalf of the victim. In the event that a person killed a member of his own family, the fine would not apply; most commonly the perpetrator was disowned and lost all legal status, property and rights.

Outlawry of this sort was tantamount to a death sentence; tribe members were required to deny a criminal any sort of food, shelter or assistance, and with no legal rights the outlaw was subject to whatever anyone felt like doing to him, without penalty.

Some injuries were exempt from this system. An opponent killed or injured in battle or a duel, or while trying to prevent a crime, would not carry a penalty. Likewise, injuries inflicted during fair play of a game or sport, or as necessary in treatment by a physician, would not be penalized. Normally any fines outstanding on an individual were considered to be void upon his death, but if he died while committing a crime his family would be liable for the fine pertaining to that offence.

Celtic laws governed who could enter into an agreement or contract, and to what value. Details varied but within the Irish system it was not legal to enter into a contract to a value greater than the individual's honour-price. A contract could be annulled by someone who would be harmed by it. For example a son whose father was about to make a bad deal that would diminish his inheritance could annul the contract, even though he could not enter into an agreement to sell or trade property he had not yet inherited.

Contracts made under duress were not considered binding, as were agreements made while drunk, except those to cooperate on the ploughing of fields. In that case it did not seem to matter how drunk the prospective ploughmen were at the time – a deal was, in that case, a deal.

The law also required everyone who owned property to give hospitality to anyone who needed it. This was subject to a reciprocal agreement not to cause trouble, and violating hospitality was considered a serious matter. So was insulting or 'satirizing' someone. Satirizing could take several forms, ranging from malicious gossip to open and unfair criticism or damaging someone's reputation by inventing a less than complimentary nickname. Even gestures could be considered satirical and carried the prospect of a fine. Speaking ill of the dead was also considered satire and required a fine to be paid to their surviving kin.

Satirizing someone could be undone by composing a poem of praise about them, and could also be used by a bard to legally shame a person of high rank into meeting their obligations. The

LEFT: **Bards had the power to improve or wreck someone's reputation with their tales and songs, but had to tread carefully when satirizing an important chieftain. Bardic satire could induce a chieftain to change his mind about an unpopular decision, or simply land the bard in trouble.**

decision as to whether a satire was legal or not was a complex one, and it would be a brave bard that satirized a powerful and bad-tempered chieftain.

Crime and Punishment

Other crimes such as theft and damage to property were also dealt with by imposing fines, which varied according to what was stolen. For most items the fine was based on twice the cost of the item stolen, modified for how far it was from his home at the time of the theft and whether violence or stealth was used. Theft of livestock such as cattle carried a higher fine, and if an item was stolen while on the land of a third party, he too had to be compensated – presumably for the damage to his reputation.

'BEING DIRTY WAS NEVER ACCEPTABLE FOR ANYONE WHO WAS NOT IN THE MIDDLE OF A FILTHY TASK.'

Trespassing by people or livestock was also punishable by a fine, although if a landowner failed to put up adequate fences he could not expect to be compensated when a neighbour's cattle wandered onto his lands. Animal trespass was considered more serious if the livestock ate grass or other fodder that could be used by the owner, or if there was damage to the ground that made it more difficult to cultivate.

However, it was considered acceptable to trespass in order to help someone in need, and stealing items that were about to be destroyed in a fire was also fair game. Corpses on the battlefield could be legally looted, and waste materials from a smithy or mill could be taken freely. There were also reduced penalties for crimes committed in honest ignorance, or from negligence without malice. Likewise, if a crime were committed because the perpetrator was in distress or under great pressure, it might be set aside without penalty.

Onlookers might be considered to be, in effect, accessories to a crime if they realized what was happening and did nothing to prevent it, while anyone offering protection or hospitality to a criminal would also be liable. However, those who had no power to prevent or interfere with a crime – such as children or persons who were infirm – would not be liable, and informing

OPPOSITE: Celtic clothing was well made and often highly decorated. Even relatively poor people apparently wore clothing of bright colours and attractive designs, and those that could afford it augmented their outfit with jewellery and accessories.

LEFT: Celtic clothing was woven on sophisticated looms, much like this modern reconstruction. A variety of fabrics were worn by people of all classes, though work clothes were probably simpler and more hard-wearing than garments for social occasions.

animal hair – including goat and badger hair. There is also strong evidence that it was not only the richer members of society that favoured fine clothing. Fibres found in mines in the Hallstatt region suggest that salt miners – traditionally not a rich man's occupation – wore brightly coloured clothing.

The Celts made good quality shoes, typically of a leather slipper type manufactured from a single piece of animal hide shaped around the foot. Evidence has been found of wooden-soled shoes and shoes with hobnails in the soles, which would make them last longer and improve grip on muddy surfaces. This was probably a necessary addition in wet northern climates.

Men typically wore long trousers or bracae, which the Romans considered noteworthy. These were often brightly coloured and were at times simply worn with a cloak that could be removed when working on a task where it might get in the way or be too warm. The trousers were sometimes accompanied by straps or wraps that bound them between the knee and ankle, presumably to prevent them from catching on anything or becoming worn.

Female clothing was typically a long dress of a sort that has become known as a 'bog dress'. This rather uncomplimentary term derives from the fact that the dress was a utility garment that was worn for all tasks, including forays out into a nearby bog to cut peat for the fire. The Celts probably had one or more terms for their dresses, but we do not know what they were.

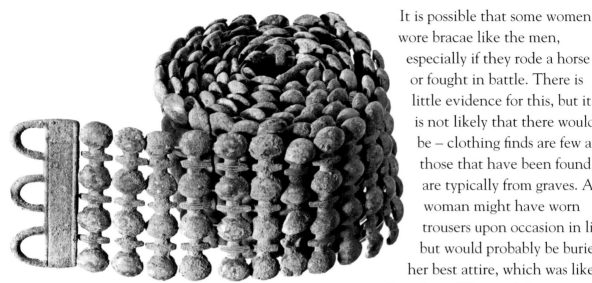

It is possible that some women wore bracae like the men, especially if they rode a horse or fought in battle. There is little evidence for this, but it is not likely that there would be – clothing finds are few and those that have been found are typically from graves. A woman might have worn trousers upon occasion in life, but would probably be buried in her best attire, which was likely to be a dress. Women did sometimes wear a shirt or tunic and a skirt, and sometimes the tunic was worn under the dress.

ABOVE: **This intricate bronze belt was produced around 800 BCE, at the beginning of the Iron Age. Although iron replaced bronze for tools and weapons, the latter remained in use for some decorative items as it was cheaper and stronger than gold.**

The tunics worn by Celtic people varied somewhat in length and design, and were somewhat indicative of status. Those that had to move freely in order to work hard would wear a relatively short tunic or shirt, while those who could afford to stand around being important were able to wear longer tunics that might come down to the knee. Tunics might or might not have sleeves, and sleeve designs may have varied according to the user's occupation. However, there is little evidence to go on as finds of male Celtic clothing are even less common than those of females.

Both genders made use of cloaks of various designs, which were sometimes woven of wool or other fabrics but might be made from leather. There is some evidence that more than one cloak might be worn; perhaps a warm cloak might be covered by one that was more waterproof when necessary. Cloaks were typically fastened with brooches, which formed part of the personal jewellery of the wearer.

Jewellery and Status Symbols

The Celts loved decorative items of gold and bronze. Some jewellery was partly functional, such as brooches and pins that kept clothing fastened. A torc around the neck was a status symbol but might also protect the neck from a blow in combat. Arm-rings seem to have been purely decorative, and would not have served as a useful form of armour.

The term torc is generally used to describe a neck ring, but it can refer to any ring of twisted metal worn around a body part such as the head, arm, neck or waist. The practice of creating them seems to date from 1200 BCE or perhaps earlier, using strips of gold hammered into a bar that was then twisted to create the characteristic design. This basic bar torc design was followed by more complex methods that created very tightly twisted torcs.

'THE CELTS CARED ABOUT THEIR STATUS IN SOCIETY AND WANTED THE RESPECT OF THEIR PEERS.'

Methods for creating torcs varied from place to place and at different times, and so did their significance. Some groups seem to have believed that the torc was not merely a symbol of warriorhood and power, but was also imbued with mystical qualities. Others seem willing to accept that being able to afford a large piece of finely worked precious metal was a status symbol in its own right.

The torc and other jewellery are typical examples of the Celtic delight with ostentation and beauty. Any given individual might have been more moved by the aesthetic qualities of finely worked gold or by the ego boost provided by showing the world his riches. Similarly, bright clothing was both a symbol of prosperity and a way of simply looking good in public.

In both cases, these decorative items played to the Celtic person's very great concern about what others thought of him. All the gold, the bright clothes, the bragging and the ostentatious hospitality add up to the same thing – the Celts cared about their status in society and wanted the respect of their peers. This was a great driving force in their society, the source of both conflict and cooperation, and helped define what it was to be a Celt.

BELOW: **Torcs, arm-rings and bracelets like this one were common in Celtic society. Decorative items might be worn as a statement of riches and status or simply because they looked good.**

3

CELTIC ART
AND RELIGION

Today, most people have an image of what Celtic art looks like.
This usually involves complex swirling patterns on rocks or
jewellery but few have any idea what these patterns mean.

The images are aesthetically pleasing and there is a strong market
for Celtic-style silver and gold jewellery. Although the ideas
that the ancient Celts were trying to symbolize may have been
forgotten, their methods at least have lived on.

Similarly, elements of Celtic religion and spirituality have
survived into the modern era in various forms. The revival – if
it can be called that – of interest in druidism in the eighteenth
century was supposedly based on Celtic practices, although in
reality neo-druidism had little more than a name in common
with its spiritual ancestor. Neo-druidism was more an invention
based on misconceptions than a real revival.

The recent increase in interest in Wicca has also brought
some Celtic concepts back to common notice. Some Wiccan
festivals are derived from Celtic predecessors, although many

OPPOSITE: **Elements
of Celtic art were
incorporated into early
Christian imagery, such
as here at the chapel of
Kilnave on the Scottish
island of Islay. Carved
crosses of this sort are
found at many locations
in Ireland and Scotland.**

cultures have similar events at the same significant times of year, and names are sometimes borrowed from traditions other than the Celtic. Wiccan marriages often use a handfasting ceremony, and some groups make use of handfasting in the traditional trial marriage or engagement context.

Other elements of Celtic mythology and art survived as folklore or influences on later traditions. Much of the art that characterized the Celtic Revival, which began in the latter half of the nineteenth century, was derived from medieval rather than Celtic-era art, but this in turn had been heavily influenced by the art of the Celtic people. A process of gradually reinterpretation and unintentional distortion has taken place, but there still exists a style that is recognized as 'Celtic' by modern people. A man or woman of 200 BCE might recognize at least some elements of this modern Celtic style.

Poetry and Music

Poetry was an important Celtic art form. It served numerous purposes, which of course included the creation of pleasing verses but also created a record of past events and a means of commentary upon current ones. Like some other cultures, the Celts preferred to store their knowledge and memories in the poems and songs of a professional group rather than commit them to writing.

A poetic rendition of events was in many ways preferable to a simple tale as the use of rhyme and meter assisted with memory. It was easier to spot mistakes or changes with a poem than a simple recital of facts, and there may have also been other factors at work too. Poetry was the specialist field of the bards, who were rigorously trained in the rules of poetry and knew how to create a suitable verse or to deliver an existing one. This ability set the bards apart from ordinary tribe members and created a measure of job security – the

BELOW: **The Turoe Stone, located in Country Galway, Ireland, is decorated in an abstract style typical of La Tène-era Celts. This originated around 500 BCE and spread across much of the Celtic world.**

fumbling efforts of those who tried to copy the bardic style ensured that everyone knew how important it was to have real bards available.

In addition to straight verse, bards had other tools at their disposal. Satire was a poetic style used to bring shame upon the victim, and in some regions a bardic satire was considered to have supernatural abilities. Indeed, there are accounts of specialist satirists who could effectively cast magic spells and curses with a well-aimed poem. Satirizing someone was a serious offence in some areas, although it is unclear whether this refers to a well-deserved bardic shaming or the more general meaning of the word. 'Satirizing', depending on context, could be anything from name-calling and rude gestures to a full-scale poem of shame.

It seems that a bardic satire had far more power than a ploughman's rude gesture, and could be used to shame a chieftain or king who was otherwise untouchable. How the bard avoided unpleasant consequences of his satire was unclear; it may be that in this case the satire was a test of public opinion. If the tribe seemed to agree with the satire, then perhaps it was a sign that they were losing confidence in their leader. In that case, a change

ABOVE: The bard was an essential part of Irish Celtic festivities, providing entertainment and perhaps some education in the form of his tales and songs. Some bards were itinerant while others were part of a chieftain's or king's household.

ABOVE: Bards were not unique to Ireland, of course. The Germanic peoples had their own bards, as depicted here, and the Skalds served a similar purpose among the Norsemen of Scandinavia.

of policy or attitude might be in order. If the satire was not well received by the tribe then it was probably unjust and the shamed chieftain might be free to respond.

A satire could be undone with a poem of praise, and these could also be used to smooth over disputes or improve relations with another sept or tribe. A good bard could command attention at the right time, perhaps distracting people from an unwise course of action or a brewing fight, and could change the mood of the gathering with his poems. He could influence policy in this way, telling carefully selected tales of vengeance, defeat or friendship to nudge those who heard in the right direction.

The bard's arsenal contained various styles of poem, using different rhyme patterns and meter, as well as song and music, to create the effects he required. The harp has become the symbol of Irish bards, and was associated with three main playing styles known as the Three Noble Strains. These would induce sadness, happiness or sleep when played correctly.

The traditional music of the Continent may have been quite different to that of the British Isles, it is difficult to say since the Celtic societies there were overlaid by Roman and later cultures. In the British Isles, Celtic music has survived

– although obviously it has also adapted and evolved over the generations – in the traditional music of Ireland, Wales, Scotland and parts of England.

Although it is easy to assume that the various forms of pipes (perhaps most famously the Highland bagpipes and Northumbrian pipes) are of Celtic origin, this may not be the case. There is some evidence of bagpipe-like instruments in great antiquity, but there is no clear indication that the Celts of the British Isles played them. However, much of the traditional pipe music that is produced today is referred to as 'Celtic' and this is probably not too inaccurate.

Whenever the pipes were adopted by any given group, they would be used to play the traditional music of those people. Their musical traditions spanned various instruments, and they would not create a whole new musical style to go with the pipes. Tunes and melodies might evolve or be adapted, but at least some elements of traditional Celtic music do live on in the guise of 'Celtic Pipes and Drums' CDs sold in tourist shops.

The Visual Art of the Celts

As with all forms of artistic expression, Celtic art was not simply invented one day. It was the product of a lengthy process of influence and development, and was subject to additional outside influences as time went on. Nor was it the preserve of specialist artists or those who created decoration for religious purposes. Art was a part of everyday life, with even quite mundane and inexpensive items receiving decoration.

The art of the ancient Celts was influenced by the people they interacted with, notably Greeks and Romans, but external concepts were usually absorbed and modified to fit with the Celts' aesthetic preferences. For example, early Celtic coins depict fairly clear images of horses, chariots and other objects, but later coins render the

BELOW: This coin was minted around 100 BCE by the Coriosolites of Armorica, on the north western coast of France. They were among the 'maritime' Celtic peoples recorded by Caesar, and probably engaged in extensive cross-channel trade.

same images in a much more abstract way. In some cases it can take some examination before the image of a powerful, galloping horse can be discerned in the swirling dots and lines of a coin.

Much of Celtic art is abstract in this manner, and while many objects are depicted it is rare to see complete human images in pre-Christian Celtic art. It is not known if there was some cultural or religious reason for this absence. Often images are surreal, depicting the closeness of the mundane world to the spiritual realms where gods, heroes and monsters dwelled.

Celtic art can thus be viewed as both mundane and religious or spiritual in nature, which is by no means a contradiction in terms. Like many ancient people the Celts lived close to nature and to their gods, and there was only a thin divide between the daily business of the farm and the settlement, and the otherworldly realms whose mysteries were revealed only to the druids.

Much Celtic art was of worked metal, notably bronze, silver and gold, and took the form of decoration on mundane items as well as items created specifically to be pleasing. Some of the latter may have been created for the purposes of trade; once the Celts discovered that others would pay in goods and coin for visually pleasing objects, there was a strong incentive to make and export them. However, it seems that the Celts liked beauty for its own sake and those that were prosperous enough would adorn themselves and their homes with jewellery and art objects.

Among the items made by Celtic craftsmen were bronze mirrors, which were often cunningly worked so that the apparently abstract decorative patterns revealed a face when the mirror was turned upside down. Faces and heads were common themes in Celtic art, and given the Celtic belief that the heads of enemies could be taken to give the

BELOW: Stones carved with strange symbols have been found all across the Celtic world. In most cases their meaning remains obscure, and all we know for certain is that it was important enough to carve into a piece of solid granite.

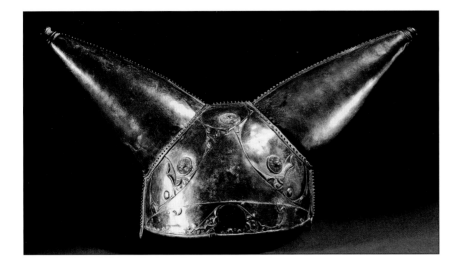

LEFT: This helmet, found in the River Thames, was probably a ceremonial item rather than being intended for use in battle. It is decorated in the La Tène style and probably dates from around 100 BCE.

user their power, they may have had connotations of strength. Stone carvings were also an important part of Celtic art. It has been suggested that stone carving was more connected with religious meanings than objects of metal. Wood may also have been extensively used, but little survives to this day.

Early Celtic art, from the Hallstatt period, did make use of straight lines but this practice faded away as time passed. By the La Tène era (500 BCE onwards) the style we would today recognize as Celtic had emerged. In general, Celtic art is characterized by a lack of simple symmetry, with complex patterns of curves and spirals covering the entire available medium. The symbolism of these patterns is highly complex, and most modern reproductions take the form of copying the general style without necessarily depicting anything in particular.

'LIKE MANY ANCIENT PEOPLES THE CELTS LIVED CLOSE TO NATURE AND TO THEIR GODS.'

However, many objects were created that did feature direct representation of people and events. These include cauldrons, helmets, mirrors and other decorated objects that offer tantalizing glimpses into the mind of the creator. In some cases it is easy to see what is being shown – a group of warriors with shields is easy to identify. Other images are more mystical or abstract, and it can be hard to tell if what is shown is a god in part-human form or a person wearing a ceremonial head-dress. These images are, in many cases, more tantalizing than the abstract patterns used in decoration, for they show us scenes of the distant past with no explanation of what we are seeing.

Celtic Myth and Religion

The Celts were a very widespread people, whose religious practices and beliefs varied over time as well as by location. Much of what we know of the Celtic gods has come down to us through the myths and traditional stories of Ireland and Wales, or has become part of other belief systems such as Romano-Celtic and later Christian religion. Thus in some cases there are numerous variants of any given story, attributing greater or lesser – or completely different – abilities and powers to any given character. Many gods and other beings had three aspects, which further confuses the issue.

Celtic myths generally agree that magical beings and gods lived apart from the mortal world in an 'Otherworld' that was known by various names. Welsh mythology frequently refers to this place as Annwyn, while Irish myths often refer to Sidhe. These tales survived long enough to be recorded in written form by the people they belonged to, or at least their descendants.

On the other hand, much of what we know about the religion of the Gallic Celts is filtered through the perception of the Roman writers that recorded it, and is inevitably distorted. Julius Caesar wrote much about what the Celts believed, but he used terms that he was familiar with. He recorded that Mercury was the chief god of the Gauls, which seems rather unlikely. It is much more probable that the Celts had a deity that fulfilled the same general functions as Mercury, and since Caesar did not know the god's actual name he used a parallel that would be familiar to his expected readership. It is possible that this is instead an example of Roman arrogance, assuming that barbarians worshipped proper Roman gods but by some other name.

The Roman assignment of parallels works as a reasonable approximation in some cases, but the Gauls had a great many gods, of whom a large proportion were associated with a fairly limited area or a specific tribe. Some of these duplicated the abilities of others and may have been absorbed into a different identity by Roman assumptions. However, as the Gauls themselves did not leave written records, the Roman accounts are in many cases the best we have to work with.

It is not unreasonable to assume that since the Celtic people spread out from a common origin and retained at least a degree of contact with one another, many apparently similar gods who have different names in different places could be the same god represented in varying ways. It is also likely that some gods were worshipped over a very large area while others were extremely localized. It follows that the more widespread gods performed functions that were relevant to everyone, while local gods were only of much importance to the tribe or region that venerated them. There is thus evidence of a general pantheon throughout the Celtic world, with local variations and additions.

Similarly, it is likely that the general format of Celtic religion was much the same throughout the Celtic world, but that local customs varied considerably from this norm at times. Caesar

OPPOSITE: A Gallo-Roman statue of the god Mercury. Identification of Celtic gods with Roman ones probably began with Roman scholars making the best interpretation they could on scanty information. After the Roman conquest of Gaul, the merging of gods became a reality.

BELOW: The enduring (if wildly incorrect) image of Celtic religion is of white-robed druids collecting mistletoe whilst surrounded by suitably savage-looking warriors.

recorded the roles – as he understood them – of Celtic religious figures. Druids were priests and also lawyers, bards recorded and recited the lore, and there were also mystical seers known as ovates or vates, although these may have been druids who were at an early stage of their careers and not fully trained, rather than a separate group. Indeed, these three groups are sometimes all considered to be druids, or at least members of the druidic social class. It is possible that the exact delineation of each group varied over time and in different places.

Celtic Gods and Goddesses

The ancient Celts worshipped gods that fulfilled the same functions as those of many other cultures. Death and life after death are important to almost all societies, and there are several Celtic gods associated with this area. Some seem to have had other responsibilities too, such as Cernunnos, who seems to be associated with both death and fertility.

Cernunnos is represented as an antlered god, and appears in many regions. More accurately, a similar antlered figure involved in similar activities appears in many areas; only in one representation is a name appended. Thus the god we know as Cernunnos might actually be several gods with different names in different regions. They seem to be fulfilling the same functions, however, so given a lack of contradicting evidence it is not unreasonable to assign the name Cernunnos to this deity whenever and wherever it appears. The same problem exists with many of the Celtic gods, especially those of Continental Europe. In many cases they are depicted but not named, forcing archeologists to take a best guess at who or what is being venerated.

Cernunnos is associated with the dead but also with nature in the form of both animals and crops. He (or another god that looks alike) is depicted on the Gundestrup Cauldron. This vessel, mostly of silver, was found in a peat bog in Denmark in 1891. Some of the images on it seem to be of mythological creatures, others are relatively mundane. As with many

'AS WITH MANY DEPICTIONS FROM CELTIC OBJECTS, INTERPRETATION IS DIFFICULT.'

depictions from Celtic objects, interpretation is difficult. In this case, Cernunnos is holding a torc in one hand and a ram-headed serpent in the other.

Another Celtic god of the dead is Sucellus, who is also associated with fertility. Sucellus is sometimes depicted as being accompanied by a three-headed dog. This representation comes from Hungary, and may indicate a connection with Cerberus, the three-headed dog-guardian of the underworld in Classical mythology. Sucellus is also depicted with a raven. Several mythologies consider ravens to be psychopomps, or guides that help the spirits of the dead find their way to the next life.

Although these death gods also seemed to have a fertility role, such as Sucellus' association with woodlands and agriculture, the Celts had several gods of healing, fertility and plenty that did not have a connection with death. A trio of mother-goddesses is depicted in various areas, sometimes accompanied by babies and

ABOVE: **This figure of an antlered man appears in several places in Celtic religious imagery. He is identified as 'Cernunnos' in one carving, and is thus generally known by that name. It is unclear whether all depictions of antlered men are the same god, however.**

ABOVE: Sucellus was a fatherly god connected with agriculture and nature. Carvings of him have been found throughout Gaul, usually holding a long-handled hammer or mallet in one hand. Sucellus often also has a pot of food or drink in his other hand, suggesting a connection with prosperity.

sometimes with fruit. Solo mother goddesses are occasionally also depicted.

Some gods of fertility and plenty are depicted without a name, often with images of fruit, wine or other foods, or with money. Roman observers often connected these gods with Mercury, and indeed frequently referred to them by that name. This can be confusing, as the Romans seem to have associated a great many Celtic gods with Mercury despite their differing representations and powers.

Naming the Gods

There are also a great many Celtic gods and goddesses associated with tribes, places and particularly bodies of water. These gods were typically worshipped in a fairly small area, and in many cases their names are not known. Roman observers associated a variety of tribal war-gods and protector-gods with their own war-god Mars, but in many cases these tribal gods were more than just a warrior god. They were the patron and protector of the tribe, which has connotations ranging from lawgiving to healing as well as protection and conflict.

Some of these local or tribal gods are known by the names of their associated tribe or region. Thus Vosegus was associated with the Vosges region of what is now France, and is connected with forests, mountains and wildlife in the region. Arduinna was a goddess with a similar function in the Ardennes region, and other deities were associated with different localities. Worship outside the associated tribe or region was probably very limited, although another area might have a virtually identical deity.

Healing deities were often associated with bodies of water or springs thought to have healing properties, including thermal springs. The goddess Sirona and the god Grannus were particularly associated with healing springs, and were worshipped over a wide area. One or both were venerated more in certain areas than others; Sirona was popular in Eastern Gaul and the Danube region, and particularly in the Moselle valley in Gaul. Grannus was particularly associated with Aquae Granni (modern-day Aachen). Some particular springs had their own local deities who might have been aspects of Sirona or Grannus, or a local and unique deity.

Some gods and goddesses are more universal than others. Belenus, whose name is given to the fire festival known as Beltane, was worshipped in much of Continental Europe under a variety of names. In Wales he was probably the god known as Beli and in Ireland as Bile, both of whom are similar. However, the Irish and Welsh aspects of this god seem to have been more associated with darkness and the underworld than with fire, as was the case with Belenus. Belenus was identified by Roman writers as Apollo.

Taranis was a thunder god primarily worshipped in Gaul and the British Isles. Symbolized by a spoked wheel and depicted as a bearded man with a thunderbolt in one hand, it is hardly surprising that Taranis was identified by Roman observers with Jupiter. As a god with power over the weather, Taranis was an important figure. Some Roman writers considered that he was one of the main Celtic gods but there are relatively few depictions of him suggesting that this may not actually be the case.

Epona was also worshipped over much of Europe as the goddess of horses. This gave her a role as both a war goddess and a fertility goddess; Epona is sometimes depicted as a mother goddess but in horse rather than human form. Epona worship spread to the British Isles and was adopted by many auxiliary cavalry units in

BELOW: The goddess Sirona was worshipped from Gaul to the Danube. She is mostly associated with healing waters, including hot springs. Images of Sirona often include eggs or serpents.

the Roman army, making Epona the only Celtic god to achieve widespread worship in the Roman Empire.

The most important of Gaulish gods – at least, according to Julius Caesar – was Lugh, after whom several towns and cities were named. These include modern Lyons in France, which was known as Lugdunum, and Carlisle in England, which was formerly known as Luguvalium. Lugh was a god of the sky or the sun, and also a patron of many skills and crafts. Roman observers identified him with both Apollo and Mercury. To the Gauls, Lugh seems to have been a leader or perhaps a king, whereas the Irish venerated him as more of a warrior god. He appears in Welsh mythology as Lleu (Lleu Llaw Gyffes). This veneration of different aspects of a god, or perhaps a change in the mythology over time, is not atypical of Celtic religion, and was perhaps inevitable as the various regions became subject to differing influences.

BELOW: **Taranis was a god of thunder worshipped across much of Europe and the British Isles. Not surprisingly, he was associated with Jupiter by Roman observers. He is usually depicted with a thunderbolt and a wheel in his hands.**

Some mythological figures seem to be considered gods at times and supernatural beings at others. The Morrigan, who appears in Irish mythology, is one such being. Variously referred to as Morrigan or The Morrigan, this sometimes-deity is a complex figure. As a goddess she is made up of three aspects, although references vary as to their identities. As a mythical being she is a shape-changer who prophesies the future and interferes in the fortunes of tribes and heroes. She is associated with conflict and rulership, and is a rather vengeful figure. She can change shape into various animals including an eel, a heifer and a raven, and can appear as a beautiful maiden or a hag depending on her purposes at the time.

Other Irish gods are less ambiguous, although it is difficult to tell if they are aspects or parallels of Continental deities or entirely unique. The Dagda was extremely important to the Celts of Ireland, not least because he led his tribe of gods and supernatural beings to conquer the previous gods of Ireland and make it available for the Celts to settle there.

The Dagda became king of his tribe, the Tuatha Dé Danann, or Tuath Dé, after his predecessor Nuada was wounded. The tribe's name means 'people of Danu' or 'tribe of the gods', and their victory led to the previous inhabitants of Ireland, known as the Fomorians, being driven away.

The Dagda's victory has parallels in the defeat of the Titans by the Greek gods and the overthrow of the Jotun (giants) by the Norse gods. It may represent the conquest of the previous inhabitants of Ireland or be symbolic of the defeat of their gods by those of the newcomers. Either way, the Dagda gave the Irish Celts a place to call home.

The Dagda had a magical hammer that could kill nine men at once, while its long handle could return them to life. This may have symbolized the power of life and death that a leader held. His magical harp had great powers to bestow order – even the seasons obeyed its music and it could be used to dictate the course of a battle. The Dagda was also associated with plenty; he had a magical cauldron that could feed anyone, and two pigs that would provide endless food.

ABOVE: Epona was associated with horses, with connotations of both war and fertility. Her worship was adopted by many Romans, notably as a patron goddess and protector of cavalrymen and their mounts.

The mother goddess of the Tuatha Dé Danann was Danu (or Dana), who is sometimes associated with the land and its rivers, and with fertility and abundance. It is possible that the river Danube was named for her, which suggests that her worship was widespread. Eventually the Tuatha Dé Danann yielded the world to mortals and went to live within the Hollow Hills or Sidhe. Thus Danu is the mother of the faerie folk.

The story of Nuada, original king of the Tuatha Dé Danann, is complex and at times contradictory. He led the Tuatha Dé

ABOVE: Although King
Nuada already had
someone at his court
who could do each of
the things Lugh offered,
there was nobody who
could do all of them.
Lugh ultimately led
the Tuatha Dé Danann
to victory over their
Fomorian enemies.

Danann in their initial attempt to gain a home in Ireland, battling the Fir Bolg who already lived there. Although the Fir Bolg were defeated, Nuada lost a hand in the battle and could no longer rule as king. His replacement was Bres, a prince of Fomorian descent, who was a harsh ruler.

Nuada, rescued from the battle by the Dagda, returned to power after being made a replacement hand out of silver, but was voluntarily succeeded by Lugh. This enabled the Tuatha Dé Danann to better resist the Fomorians led by Bres and his ally Balor. Nuada was killed in battle against the Fomorians but was avenged by Lugh.

The ancient Celts had many other gods and goddesses, some of whom were of only regional importance. It is likely that many could be considered alternate local identities of deities venerated elsewhere or more generally. Some of the Celtic deities survived into the Christian era as saints, while others became associated with opposition to Christianity. For example the image of Cernunnos, the wild antlered god, is sometimes associated with devil worship.

Festivals and Holy Days

Many of the Celtic holy festivals have continued to be observed, in one form or another, to the present day. The rise of Christianity and other religions did not eradicate these 'pagan' festivals so much as co-opt them – as indeed it is possible that the Celts co-opted the festivals of other belief systems. This is not least because Celtic festivals tended to take place at times of the year – spring, midwinter and so forth – that are significant to people of almost any culture.

Habit also played a part; it made sense for emerging religions to hold their festivals on days that were already special. This not only made the transition to the new religion's festivals easier for its devotees, but also helped drive out old beliefs as the faithful could only attend one festival at a time.

Today, there are many who maintain that the Celtic New Year began with the festival of Samhain on the night of 31 October/1 November. This is not borne out by evidence that survives from the medieval period and from Welsh legends, in which various New Year celebrations take place in the depths of winter. Be that as it may, Samhain was one of the most important – if not the most important – of the Celtic festivals.

The festival of Samhain took place at the midpoint between the autumn equinox and the winter solstice and was associated with the end of the summer and preparations for the coming winter. There were also connotations of death, with feasts to honour the dead. It is not clear whether or not the ancient Celts believed that the barriers between the lands of the living and the dead grew thin at this time, although there are records from the medieval period of a belief that the faerie folk were active at this

BELOW: **The Grianan of Aileach is a ringfort dating from 600–700 CE, though it is likely that the site was in use long before this. The fort was both a centre of political power and also an important religious site.**

time. Exactly how what was probably a harvest/preparation for winter festival became distorted into the modern holiday that takes place on the same date is open to some conjecture.

The midwinter festival, Yule, traditionally took place on the winter solstice (21 December) and was probably connected with the sun gods. It is a more likely candidate than Samhain for the beginning of a new year, as it symbolized the return of light and warmth to the world. The tradition of the Yule log is derived from the belief that the sun stood still for 12 days at this time of year; the log was burned to provide light and heat in its absence. Surviving traditions in some areas also involve torchlight processions and the burning of juniper to usher in the return of the light and to drive out evil, which again makes a logical connection with the festival signifying a new beginning.

The midpoint between winter solstice and spring equinox, 2 February in the modern calendar, was another fire festival. Known as Imbolc, this festival celebrated the beginning of spring and was traditionally the day when milking of ewes began. Imbolc was co-opted by the Christian faith, along with Yule, and is now Candlemas. The day is also associated with St Brigid, who may have originally been a Celtic goddess that gradually

BELOW: Modern-day druids gather at Stonehenge to celebrate the spring equinox. Stonehenge predates the 'Celtic Era' by many centuries, but so do the Celtic festivals – the same key points in the natural year have been considered auspicious throughout human history.

morphed into a Christian saint. If so, then Imbolc may have been associated with her worship, at least in some areas.

The first day of spring, falling on the spring equinox, was the day of Ostara – Easter in the modern calendar. The day and night being exactly the same length may have been taken to symbolize a balance in nature or between good and evil, making this day extremely significant. Ostara was a day to hope and pray for a prosperous year, especially in terms of agriculture and livestock. It was also the beginning of the planting season, and thus a significant landmark in the mundane calendar.

Beltaine, which fell midway between the spring equinox and the summer solstice, was in many ways the opposite of Samhain. It was a fire festival, associated with good luck in the coming months. The origins of the festival's name are unclear – it may be associated with the god Belenus or even the Old Testament god Baal. As part of the festival, cattle were driven between large fires, or people walked between them. This was to drive out evil influences and ensure good health and luck in the coming summer.

Beltaine is the beginning of the summer, an auspicious time for handfasting and marriage, and has survived to modern times as May Day. This time of year is extremely significant to agricultural societies in particular, so it is hardly surprising that the festival was continued after the end of the Celtic era. Similarly, there seem to have been fire festivals at midsummer in at least some Celtic areas. These include Ireland and perhaps the Orkney and Shetland islands, but there is less evidence of such activity in Wales and much of Scotland.

The beginning of autumn was celebrated by the festival of Lammas, or Lughnasa. The name derives from Lugh, the Irish sun god, and the festival was connected with a celebration of the

ABOVE: **Beltaine marked the beginning of the growing season. Celebrations involved the use of fire to drive out evil and bad luck, ensuring a prosperous summer. Rituals also involved protection against witchcraft and the malice of supernatural beings.**

harvest as well as sorrow at the end of the summer. From Lughnasa onwards the year became colder and darker, leading to the hard times of winter. The end of the harvest season was celebrated on the autumn equinox, in September, with the festival of Mabon.

As with the spring equinox, this was considered a magical time as day and night were of equal length.

There are many legends that these festivals were mystically significant times, at which the faerie folk could cross into the mundane world and heroes might do great deeds. However, the festivals might have been simply landmarks in some of the hero-tales, giving the deeds of the protagonists both a context in terms of when in the year they took place and also a greater significance due to association with important dates.

Be that as it may, the great Celtic festivals took place at obvious and logical times of the year, and it is hardly surprising that they were co-opted by later religions or became socially important dates even for those who considered them to have no religious or spiritual significance.

'OBSERVERS NOTED THAT AT TIMES LIVE ANIMALS WOULD BE THROWN ONTO THE FUNERAL PYRE.'

Life After Death

The ancient Celts had a strong belief in the idea of life after death. They believed that the dead would live other lives, and that some things could be taken into that life. This included goods and wealth, but also in some cases debts. It was common for people to be buried with significant wealth or useful goods, and Celtic burials have been found that included quite large quantities of wine. Where cremation was used, observers noted that at times live animals would be thrown onto the funeral pyre. This presumably ensured that they accompanied their owner into their next existence.

Burials have been found in which apparent family members were interred together. While it is possible that a husband and wife met their end together, it is more likely that at times hostages, captives or even family members were killed and buried with an important person. The discovery of decapitated (and in some cases bound) skeletons buried without grave-goods around someone interred with rich possessions suggests the sacrifice of captive enemies with a warrior or leader.

Burials of warriors often included armour and weapons, and often the warrior was placed facing the lands of enemy tribes or nations. The warrior could then keep watch even in death, perhaps from a high burial mound, and might spring from the grave to defend his family and tribe from assault if needed.

Roman and other sources record that the Celts believed that souls would survive the death of the body, and attributed to this belief the general disregard that many Celtic warriors had for their own safety. The souls of the dead would pass into new bodies in another world (or perhaps another part of this world) and begin another life, although with the same identity. This meant that a debt unpaid in this life would carry over and be settled at some point, and more importantly that each person was effectively immortal.

The world that the dead entered was not some dismal Hades or grey waiting-place; it was another world as rich and fascinating

BELOW: The ancient Celts believed that after death they passed on to a new life elsewhere. Grave-goods allowed them to take some of their wealth with them, which was only fair since unpaid debts were also carried over into the next life.

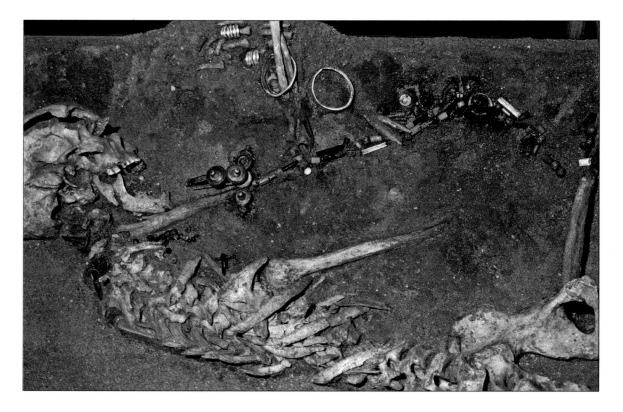

as the one the departed had just left. Some writers recorded that the Celts thought that sometimes the next life might be in animal form, but this is doubtful or possibly a local variation. There are also accounts of the dead returning as ghosts or spectres, but these may be later interpretations of Celtic legends. For the most part, when the dead do return in stories, they do so as people who seem to be very much alive.

The Returned

The returned dead, according to Celtic legends, could engage in most activities that a living person might. They could assist a hero in a fight or seduce someone's wife. They could eat and drink, and would easily pass for a living person. However, the dead also had supernatural powers shared by gods and the faerie folk, and could become invisible or travel from place to place without anyone witnessing how.

Some of the traditional Celtic burial customs were designed to prevent the dead from wandering around the countryside. Large stones placed over the grave, or the practice of tying the limbs of the departed, were intended to restrict the activities of the corpse. Even so, it was still sometimes possible to obtain information from the dead, often by visiting or even sleeping in their tombs at night.

BELOW: Chun Quoit is a fine example of a dolmen, or portal tomb. The huge stones were originally set in an earth mound which has since eroded away. Chun Quoit was constructed around 2400 BCE, possibly by early proto-Celtic people.

Exactly where the dead went when they were not returning to help out or plague the living is unclear. Translations of Celtic beliefs have become distorted by the perceptions and misconceptions of those that recorded them. Some writers claim that the Celts believed in a mystical island where the dead – or perhaps some of them – went, while others refer to having to cross an underground ocean. There

are references to the dead dwelling underground, but if this is the case then such a realm might have been much more cheerful than the underground hells of other cultures.

It is not even clear if the Celts believed that their new lives took place in another world or a different part of the same one, nor if it mattered. What is important is that they believed that death was not the end but simply an interruption before life continued somewhere else. For this reason death in battle was not something to be greatly feared and suicide might actually be a good option if it allowed escape from a desperate or miserable situation.

It does seem that Celtic beliefs baffled and confused many observers, who tried to equate them to other belief systems and in so doing muddied the waters for future scholars. Their beliefs were, like many other aspects of their culture, unique and not really explainable in terms of someone else's religion. Inference and conjecture can only go so far, and unfortunately the people who really understood it all passed on to another life somewhere else long ago.

ABOVE: **A Celtic funeral was an important affair for the dead as well as the living. The deceased might decide to return and plague their neighbours or relatives if not properly sealed within the tomb.**

4

CELTIC MYTHS AND LEGENDS

Most of the myths known to us today were passed down through folklore and have naturally become distorted. Others were told over the generations and survived long enough to be recorded in medieval times.

However, the literate class of that era were of course mostly Christian monks, who most definitely had an agenda. Thus it is not possible to say with certainty that the stories told today are an accurate version of the originals – indeed, it is quite likely that many of the versions told in the Celtic era were 'enhanced' along the way by the bards that retold them.

Although the myths, legends and stories of the European Celts are largely lost to us, some elements may have survived in the stories passed down in Ireland, Wales and other areas that escaped Roman conquest. Many of these legends revolve around the adventures of heroes and their interactions with the gods or other supernatural beings. Some of these tales are obviously

OPPOSITE: Although referred to as a Janus stone because it has two faces, this statue on Boa Island is not a representation of the Roman god Janus. Which of the Celtic gods or goddesses it represents is not known today.

myths, while others contain tantalizing elements of real history that can be corroborated by other sources.

Irish myths seem to indicate that the Celts found opposition when they arrived in what would someday be Ireland. This opposition took the form of a race known as the Fomorians, who are represented as wild and savage. Fomorians are sometimes depicted as human, sometimes with a goat's head, and at times as strange beings with only one arm and one leg.

As the opponents of the Tuatha Dé Danann, the Tribe of Danu (i.e. the Celts), the Fomorians are naturally depicted as treacherous, evil and lacking any sort of redeeming features. It is not clear who the Fomorians actually were; they may have been the previous inhabitants of Ireland or perhaps an earlier wave of arrivals. It is possible that the struggles between the Tuatha Dé Danann and the Fomorians was more symbolic of the clash between belief systems of new arrivals and original inhabitants than a record of conflict in the mortal world.

The Book of Invasions (or *Book of Conquests*) forms part of the Mythological Cycle, which collectively describes the body of traditional lore and tales making up Irish Celtic mythology. The *Book of Invasions* deals with five invasions (or perhaps migrations) into Ireland by successive waves of Celtic people, culminating in the surviving Celtic culture there. These mythological invasions have parallels in known events, but the correlation is not exact. In all probability there was considerable movement between Ireland and other parts of Europe, especially while the land bridge

BELOW: **The fort at Dun Aonghasa (Dun Aengus) in Galway, Ireland, was originally constructed around 1100 BCE. The defences were greatly augmented about 500 years later. According to legend it was built by the Fir Bolg as a refuge after their defeat by the Tuatha Dé Danann.**

LEFT: Very little is known for sure about the people normally referred to as Picts. They had much in common with the ancient Celts and may have been a Celtic group with some regional variations, which gradually merged into later Caledonian cultures.

to mainland Britain existed. It is possible that the Picts, normally associated with Scotland, may have lived in Ireland as well, and groups could easily have crossed from northern Gaul or Iberia.

According to ancient scholars, the Iverni tribe crossed into Britain, followed later by the Belgae from Gaul and the Lagin from Brittany. The Féni were the last group of invaders, and are generally thought to be the people referred to as Milesians in the *Book of Invasions*. It is these people who created the Celtic culture that survived in Ireland.

Invasion Stories

The earliest arrivals in Ireland were led by Cesair, who according to the Christian chroniclers that recorded the tale was a granddaughter of Noah. Forbidden to board the Ark, Cesair led a small band of people to seek a sanctuary and found Ireland to be very suitable. There were three men and 50 women in Cesair's band, and originally the plan was to divide the land up among the men and populate it with their children.

Cesair chose one of the men, Fintan Mac Bochra, as her husband, and presumably took better care of him than the other men received; both of them died. Fintan now essentially had 50 wives, a situation that he did not find agreeable. Turning himself into a salmon, Fintan Mac Bochra left Ireland and Cesair died of a broken heart. The fate of the other women

ABOVE: **Tuan's ability to take on the form of animals allowed him to escape his enemies many times but eventually proved his undoing. He was caught and eaten whilst he was in the form of a salmon.**

is not known, but they evidently failed to find new husbands.

Cesair was probably a Celtic cultural hero before the Christian scholars rewrote her backstory and turned her into a Biblical character. This process was not uncommon; several Celtic gods and heroes found a new career as Christian saints, and many survive in this form.

Cesair's attempt to settle Ireland was obviously unsuccessful; there was no sign of Cesair's people when the next invaders arrived. These were led by Partholon, and apparently came from Greece by way of a roundabout route. The Partholonians were the first arrivals in Ireland after the Great Flood, arriving three centuries after Cesair's ill-fated band.

Partholon had been exiled from Greece for murdering his parents, although he had lost an eye in the process, and led his band of wanderers for seven years before they settled in Ireland. There, it was only three years before Partholon and his people got into trouble with the locals. This is the first appearance of the Fomorians, who are described as having only one arm and one leg. Despite this, they proved dangerous foes and were defeated only after a hard fight.

Partholon drove the Fomorians from Ireland, although it is not certain where they went. Nor is it recorded where they came from in the first place; they were not encountered in the time of Cesair so presumably arrived in the 312 years that elapsed between the first and second invasions. Later stories place the Fomorians' stronghold on Toraigh (Tory) island off the north-west coast of Ireland, so perhaps they were never inhabitants at all, merely raiders and troublemakers.

The Partholonians were ruled by Partholon for about 30 years after their victory, and lasted for a total of 120 years before succumbing to plague. The only survivor was Tuan, who must have possessed magical powers as he was Partholon's nephew and thus of great age when the rest of the Partholonians died out. Tuan lived alone for 30 more years before more invaders arrived, and evaded them by turning himself into animals including a stag, an eagle, a boar and a salmon. It was while in the latter form that he was caught and eaten by one of the new arrivals.

These new invaders were led by Nemed, who was descended from one of Noah's sons, and thus became known as the Nemedians. Their origins are unclear; the Nemedians are variously described as coming from the west and from Iberia, and they apparently wandered the oceans in a fleet of 32 ships for 18 months before landing in Ireland.

The Nemedians settled in Ireland and initially seemed to do quite well. The wife of a man named Cairill became pregnant after eating a salmon that she presumably did not know was Tuan in animal form. The son she gave birth to was named Tuan Mac Cairill, and became the author of the *Book of Invasions*. The fact that the child retained Tuan's name suggests powerful magic at work and possibly some kind of reincarnation.

However, the Nemedians soon found themselves in conflict with the Fomorians, who had presumably returned after Partholon's people died out. The Nemedians were victorious

LEFT: **Toraigh (or Tory Island), was the stronghold of the evil Fomorians. Their fortress was a tower built on the highest point of the island, and it features in several heroic tales.**

over the Fomorians but suffered badly in their wars. Plague also took its toll and the weakened Nemedians were oppressed by the Fomorians for many years.

The Nemedians eventually tired of paying tribute to their Fomorian overlords and rebelled, defeating the Fomorians and driving them back to Toraigh Island. There, the Nemedians won a final victory at such great cost that only 30 of them remained alive afterwards.

'INITIALLY THE TWO GROUPS AGREED TO LIVE IN PEACE, BUT THE FIR BOLGS CHANGED THEIR MINDS.'

Some of the Nemedians left Ireland for other lands. These included Britán Máel, from whom the name 'Britain' is said to be derived, and his father Fergus Lethderg. They settled in Alba (Scotland) with some of their followers, while others managed to travel all the way to Greece. There, they were enslaved. A group managed to reach safety in the far north, although exactly where they ended up is not known. They would eventually become the Tuatha Dé Danann and return to Ireland.

The enslaved Nemedians became known as 'bag men' as their work was to carry bags of soil to areas where there was little, increasing the fertility of otherwise rocky Thracian hillsides. These 'bag men', or Fir Bolg, eventually revolted, made boats out of their soil bags and somehow managed to sail all the way back to Ireland.

The returning Nemedians, now known as Fir Bolg, resettled in Ireland and spread out across the land, although inevitably there was conflict. Some accounts speak of battles with the Fomorians, while others say that the Fir Bolg were driven from much of their territory by a new wave of invaders. These were the Tuatha Dé Danann, returning like the Fir Bolg to the lands of their ancestors.

Tribal Conflicts

Initially the two groups agreed to live in peace, but the Fir Bolgs changed their minds and made war upon the Tuatha Dé Danann. The resulting Battle of Magh Tuireadh was extremely bloody, with great loss on both sides. The Tuatha Dé Danann had an advantage over the Fir Bolgs in that they possessed superior technology, notably in terms of weapons and armour, and ultimately the Fir Bolgs were defeated.

Both sides lost their kings in the battle. Eochaid Mac Eirc, king of the Fir Bolgs, was slain while Nuada, leader of the Tuatha Dé Danann, lost his hand in battle with the Fir Bolg, which meant he could no longer be king. The defeated Fir Bolg took refuge on the Aran islands in what is now County Galway. According to legend they built a great fortress there, Dún Aonghasa. This fort exists, and its original construction is dated to around 1100 BCE. The fortress was greatly expanded later, probably during the Iron Age, creating one of the most impressive 'primitive' fortifications in the world.

The Tuatha Dé Danann allowed the Fir Bolgs to retain the province of Connaught, and interacted with them peacefully. Tailtiu, widow of the king of the Fir Bolgs, married a Tuatha Dé Danann warrior and became foster-mother to the god Lugh. Tailtiu was the daughter of a foreign king, probably from Iberia. She worked herself to death to improve the fertility of Ireland, and is honroured along with Lugh at the festival of Lughnasa.

Having defeated the Fir Bolgs at the first battle of Magh Tuireadh, the Tuatha Dé Danann had to find a new king to replace Nuada. They elected Bres, who was the son of a Tuatha Dé Danann woman and Elatha, king of the Fomorians. The Tuatha Dé Danann had made peace with the Fomorians and

ABOVE: **Dún Aonghasa is considered one of the most impressive 'barbarian' fortifications in the world, though its primary purpose was more likely religious than military. It has been partially rebuilt as a heritage site.**

ABOVE: Despite being held in a tower on Tory Island, Ethlinn (Daughter of the Fomorian king Balor) was visited by Cian of the Tuatha Dé Danann. Their surviving child was Lugh, who would eventually slay Balor.

initially had no dispute with them, but the events of Bres' rule changed that.

Bres was a god of agriculture, and out of his depth as a king. His rule was unwise, harsh and eventually tyrannical to the point that the Tuatha Dé Danann decided to overthrow him. The healer god Dian Cécht made Nuada a new hand out of silver, but since he was still missing his real hand Nuada could not be king.

Later, Nuada received a new arm of flesh and blood (or possibly regrew his old one) from Miach, which sent Dian Cécht into a jealous rage. Dian Cécht murdered Miach in retribution for outdoing him, but in the meantime he helped the Tuatha Dé Danann defeat the Fomorians by creating magic waters that would restore health and heal wounds if the warriors bathed in them.

More importantly, since he was whole again, Nuada could be restored to rulership. This pleased the Tuatha Dé Danann, who overthrew the tyrannical Bres. The Fomorians were less impressed, and their leader, Balor, decided to assist Bres in regaining his throne. As well as might and savagery the Fomorians resorted to trickery and deceit; Bres' son Ruadan disguised himself to gain the opportunity to slay the Tuatha Dé Danann smith-god, Goibhniu. This deprived the tribe of repairs to their weapons at a time when they were most needed. The healing waters were also destroyed by a Fomorian stealth attack.

Backed by his Fomorian allies, Bres struck while the Tuatha Dé Danann were weakened, and slew both Nuada and his wife Macha, goddess of warriors. The assistance of Balor was of paramount importance to Bres; known as Balor of the Evil Eye, Balor could kill with just his gaze.

In the hour of greatest need, the Tuatha Dé Danann received aid from Lugh Lámhfada, or Lugh of the Long Hand. Lugh was one of triplets borne by Ethlinn, daughter of Balor. His father was Cian, son of Danu and Dian Cécht. With this impressive if mixed lineage, Lugh and his siblings were destined for greatness. However, Balor had heard that the child of Ethlinn would eventually kill him, and having failed to prevent her meeting Lugh's father, Balor had ordered the children slain. Only Lugh survived, to be rescued and raised by the Tuatha Dé Danann. Lugh was taught by his uncle Goibhniu the smith, and Tailtiu was his foster-mother.

Skilled in all the Arts

In his new home, Lugh learned a great deal and became known as Lugh Samildánach: 'skilled in all the arts'. These included combat as well as the skills of the bard, the physician, the smith and the carpenter. He demonstrated his skills and his great strength to the Tuatha Dé Danann, and was highly regarded for his abilities as well as the four great treasures he acquired. These included a magical sword and spear, a stone that revealed the true king or Ireland, and a cauldron that could feed everyone without becoming empty.

Lugh's greatest service to the Tuatha Dé Danann, however, was his defeat of Balor. As nine attendants held open Balor's huge single eye, allowing his killing gaze to fall upon the Tuatha Dé Danann, Lugh launched a stone at it with his sling, knocking it out. The eye slew 27 Fomorian warriors even as it lay on the ground. This turned the tide of battle and the Fomorians were defeated. They were forced to accept the Tuatha Dé Danann as lords of Ireland and to retreat to their island, although Lugh spared Bres in return for his knowledge of agriculture.

BELOW: The name of Mil Espaine (or Milesius) derives from the Latin for 'Hispanic Soldier'. His sons conquered Ireland, driving out the Tuatha Dé Danann, and took the land for their own. This makes Mil Espaine the mythological ancestor of all modern Irish people.

Lugh became king of Ireland for the next four decades and took several wives. One of them was seduced by Cermait, and Lugh slew him in revenge. Cermait's sons sought vengeance and eventually killed Lugh, at which time he had ruled for 40 prosperous and reasonably peaceful years. He was succeeded by Dagda, Cermait's father, who ruled for another 80 years despite a mortal wound taken in battle against the Fomorians.

Dagda's sons ruled Ireland until the Milesians arrived. This was a tribe led by Mil Espaine, who had come from Scythia by way of Egypt and finally Iberia before landing in Ireland. Relations were at first peaceful but conflict broke out between the Milesians and the Tuatha Dé Danann over a misunderstanding that escalated into a war.

The Milesians sent a fleet of 65 ships against the Tuatha Dé Danann, who tried to forestall the invasion using magic. Although they summoned a fog and tried to make the Milesian ships go astray, the Tuatha Dé Danann were thwarted by the magic of the bard Amairgin, Mil's son. An attempt to sink the Milesians' ships with a magical storm also failed, and they were able to land their army in Ireland.

It was now that Ireland acquired its magical name, Erin. The Tuatha Dé Danann were at that time ruled by the three sons of Dagda, whose wives met with the Milesians. Each asked for them to give Ireland her name, and Eriu, wife of MacGreine was chosen for the honour. In return she assisted the Milesians, who defeated the Tuatha Dé Danann in battle and gained control of Ireland, or Erin as they called it. All three kings of the Tuatha Dé Danann and their wives were killed in the conflict with the Milesians, but the Tuatha Dé Danann escaped destruction. The tribe retreated to secret places hidden by magic and became magical and immortal,

BELOW: **Mannanán Mac Lir is associated with both the sea and the underworld. He had many magical treasures, and gifted several to other prominent figures including Lugh. Among them was Mac Lir's sword Answerer, which gave wounds that didn't ever heal.**

LEFT: This gold model of a ship is part of a hoard found in Broighter, Northern Ireland, in 1896. It is thought to be a votive honouring Mannanán Mac Lir. Other finds at the same site included a gold torc and bowl.

perhaps god-like beings who at times came out from the Sidhe to assist or hinder mortals. Thus the Milesians gained control of Ireland and became the ancestors of the later Celtic people there.

The Tuatha Dé Danann were led into the Otherworld (Sidhe) by Mannanán Mac Lir, a sea-god who also had powers of magic, healing and control over the weather. Mannanán Mac Lir is sometimes considered to be the father of Lugh's foster-mother Tailtiu; in other accounts her father is a king in Iberia. Mannanán Mac Lir had a magical ship called *Wave-Sweeper*, although he sometimes travelled by chariot over water.

Mannanán Mac Lir lived in a place usually referred to as the Land of Youth, and it was here that he took the Tuatha Dé Danann when the Milesians defeated them. They were made immortal by eating Mannanán's magical pigs, which could be killed, roasted and eaten every day but came back to life in time for the next.

Battle Stories

Many of the Irish myths revolve around great battles, feuds or the deeds of heroes. Some of these were rather personal or even petty affairs, while others were world changing in their consequence.

For example, the first battle of Magh Tiuregh saw the Tuatha Dé Danann defeat the Fir Bolg and drive them into far corners of Ireland. This was a politically significant victory, but the second battle fought on the same spot was rather different.

The Fomorians were a mortal enemy who had oppressed the Tuatha Dé Danann. They are normally described and depicted as misshapen, evil and strange, agents of darkness whereas Lugh was a heroic warrior who brought light. The victory of the Tuatha Dé Danann over their Fomorian foes was a triumph of the sun-god Lugh over the forces of darkness, with great mythic significance.

The victory was hard won, however. Lugh's first attempt at making preparations for the revolt against Fomorian rule, resulted in the death of his father, Cian. On the way to gather warriors for the coming battle, Cian was attacked by the sons of Turenne, who slew him as their families were in a blood feud. Cian tried to hide from the brothers by taking on the form of a pig, but was discovered and fatally wounded. The brothers were merciful enough to grant his final wish – to return to his normal form and die as a man.

Perhaps because the incident resulted in a recognizable body rather than a dead pig, the deed was discovered and Lugh

BELOW: **The Stone of Destiny stands atop the hill of Tara, in County Meath. The immediate area has been inhabited since Neolithic times, and was fortified during the Iron Age. Tradition holds that this is the seat of the High Kings of Ireland.**

captured the brothers. Lugh offered the murderers a choice between execution for their crime and a set of nigh-impossible quests that would gather assistance for the war.

The brothers were successful in most of their quests, and brought Lugh a magical spear that would take flight and attack the enemy on its own as well as a pigskin that would heal any wound. The brothers were gravely wounded in their efforts and asked Lugh to use the pigskin to heal them. He refused, taking vengeance for the slaying of his father.

In the meantime, Dagda was also busy making preparations. Dagda is a purely Irish god, extremely important in Irish myths but not worshipped elsewhere. His name means 'good god' and he was also known as 'lord of great knowledge' and 'father of all'. Myths vary as to Dagda's origins, but he was a child of Danu and probably brother to Nuada, king of the Tuatha Dé Danann.

Dagda possessed several magical treasures and obtained others in time for the battle, but once the seven-year preparations for the revolt were made, he set out to obtain information about the Fomorians' plans while Lugh mustered the Tuatha Dé Danann for battle. On the night of Samhain, Dagda encountered a woman who turned out to be The Morrigan. From her he learned of the Fomorians' plans.

Morrigan, sometimes referred to as The Morrigan, was a rather complex goddess, or perhaps an equally complex composite of three goddesses. She represented sovereignty over Ireland as well as fertility and war, and is sometimes called queen of demons. Morrigan could also prophesy the future, and after sleeping with Dagda she used this power to tell him what the Fomorians would do. She also agreed to use her powers against them in battle.

'HE WENT TO MEET WITH THE FOMORIANS UNDER A FLAG OF TRUCE, HOPING TO MISLEAD THEM.'

Morrigan became one of Dagda's wives, and in order to ensure that Ireland remained fertile, he was required to sleep with her every Samhain. In the meantime, he went to meet with the Fomorians under a flag of truce, hoping to mislead them and buy some more time for his people to make ready for war. The Fomorians tricked Dagda by creating a deep pit filled with porridge and challenging him to eat it all. If he did so, they would release him.

Dagda won his release by eating all the porridge, and the Fomorians kept their word, but he was so bloated that he made a comical sight lurching along with a vastly distended belly. It was in this uncomfortable form that he met the daughter of Indech, one of the Fomorian kings. Dagda found her attractive but this was not reciprocated; indeed she attacked him, then demanded that he carry her home. This was something of a struggle, and along the way Dagda lost his bloated appearance. When not full of porridge, Dagda was an attractive man, and the two became lovers. She tried to convince Dagda not to go against the Fomorians, but he was adamant and eventually she agreed to help him with magic.

With these preparations made, the Tuatha Dé Danann were able to confront the Fomorians and inflict a permanent defeat. Despite an attempt on the life of Goibhniu the smith by Ruadan, son of the Tuatha Dé Danann's Fomorian-puppet king, the tribe of Danu were able to put up a good fight. However, with many of their number (including their reinstalled King Nuada) slain by Balor's evil eye the battle was in grave doubt.

The intervention of Dagda's allies, including Morrigan, was significant, but it was not until Lugh entered the fight that victory was assured. Initially kept out of the battle in the hope of keeping him safe, Lugh arrived in time to knock out Balor's evil eye with a slingstone. Dagda had been given a mortal wound by Balor's wife – some accounts say he died on the field – but despite this he was able to become king after Lugh and ruled for many years.

After the death of Balor, the Fomorians came off rather badly. Some were able to steal Dagda's harp and escape from the battle. Dagda followed them and called the harp to him; it crushed several Fomorian warriors in its flight, after which Dagda used its magic to allow his few companions to escape from the Fomorians. He played the first of the Three Noble Strains and made everyone very sad, then the second to make them forget the war as they laughed. Last, Dagda played the strains that caused everyone to fall asleep, and he and his companions slipped away.

Dagda apparently ruled over a time of relative peace and prosperity after the defeat of the Fomorians. This may have been partially secured by his wisdom in letting King Bres live in return for his knowledge of agriculture. About 50 years after his death the Milesians arrived and drove the Tuatha Dé Danann into their supernatural hiding-place, and ushered in a new era of Irish history.

Hero Stories

The stories of the Tuatha Dé Danann belong to the first set of Celtic myths, often referred to as the *Book of Invasions* or the Mythological Cycle. Later tales are generally grouped into the Ulaid Cycle (also known as the Ulster Cycle or Red Branch Cycle) and the Fenian Cycle (also known as the Ossianic Cycle). These groupings are the work of later writers and scholars, and other groupings have been suggested as well as many tales that do not seem to fit anywhere in particular.

The greatest of the Celtic heroes after the 'mythological' era was Cú Chullain, a member of the famous Red Branch order of warriors. The Ulaid Cycle is largely concerned with the adventures of these warriors and particularly Cú Chullain.

Like many heroes, Cú Chullain had a suitably mysterious origin. The druid Cathbad, while searching for one of his daughters who had vanished along with her entourage, chanced upon her as his party sought shelter from a storm. His daughter was with a member of the Tuatha Dé Danann, Lugh Lamfada, and she had a child by him. The child was initially named Sétanta, but earned the title Cú Chullain when still a boy.

Sétanta had been playing hurley, and when he finished he went to join

BELOW: The sorceress Morgana le Fay of the Arthurian legends is derived from the Morrigan, a Celtic goddess with multiple aspects. The Morrigan is a vicious enemy and a powerful friend, but is not always reliably one or the other.

ABOVE: Cú Chulainn earned his name, which means 'hound of Culann' from the time he spent guarding the house of Culann the smith while a replacement for the guard dog he had slain was trained.

King Cathbad's household at the home of Culann, a master smith. Culann had a fearsome guard dog, which attacked the boy. He defended himself with his hurley stick and slew the hound. Culann was dismayed at the death of his dog, so Sétanta offered to guard his house for a year and to train a replacement guard dog. For this he was given the name Cú Chullain, meaning hound of Culann.

Cú Chullain's career as a hero began, not atypically, with him trying to impress a girl. Emer, a chieftain's daughter, proclaimed that she would not marry a man who had not performed heroic deeds. Cú Chullain set off for the Isle of Skye to obtain training that would allow him to do so, but to even qualify for the training he had to perform incredible feats. Among these was the Bridge of Leap, which required the warrior to cross a gorge by jumping onto a moving platform and then leaping to the far side. Cú Chullain managed on the fourth try and qualified for training.

Among the feats that Cú Chullain learned to perform was the gae bolg, the trick of throwing a many-barbed spear with the toes, but before he had completed his training his mentor was challenged by the female warrior Aife, and Cú Chullain went along to help. He challenged Aife to single combat and was obviously overmatched, but distracted her by telling Aife that her chariot horses were injured. He thus gained the upper hand but agreed not to kill Aife if she in turn agreed to end the quarrel. Cú Chullain and Aife then became lovers, and had a son named Connla.

Cú Chullain returned to Ireland where his berserker rage made him both a tremendous warrior and a liability to his friends. As he returned from battle, still raging and liable to kill anyone he met, the king ordered several women to greet him naked. This caused Cú Chullain some embarrassment, and while he was confused he was grabbed and repeatedly plunged into a cauldron of water. The water boiled and the cauldron burst, but Cú Chullain was cooled off enough to cease berserking.

Cú Chullain's berserker rage was a terrible thing, warping him into a grotesque mass of muscle and sinew that revolved furiously inside his skin. His lungs and liver were in his throat, and his feet and knees turned backwards. He fought surrounded by a black mist of his own blood that spouted from his forehead. In this form, sometimes described as the Torque, he was unstoppable and invincible. The only man ever to face Cú Chullain's berserker rage survived only because the hero chose not to kill him. Cú Chullain picked the warrior up and shook him until he broke, then left him to live in pain rather than finishing him off.

The most famous of Cú Chullain's exploits is told in the tale of the cattle raid of Cooley. This arose out of an inequality of the wealth of Queen Medb of Connacht and her husband Ailill. Both were equal, which was desirable in a Celtic marriage, except that Medb had owned Finnbennach, an extremely virile white-horned bull. Finnbennach was now owned by her husband, apparently by the bull's choice of allegiance, and this made her inferior in wealth. She sent emissaries to trade for a loan of the equally impressive brown bull of Cooley.

Negotiations with the Ulstermen, who owned the brown bull, went badly and Medb decided to take the bull by force. She sent an army into Ulster, whose men were at the time incapacitated by a curse originating from an unwise bet. Although heavily pregnant, a woman named Macha was forced to race the king's chariot to prove her husband's boasts were true. She gave birth after the race and

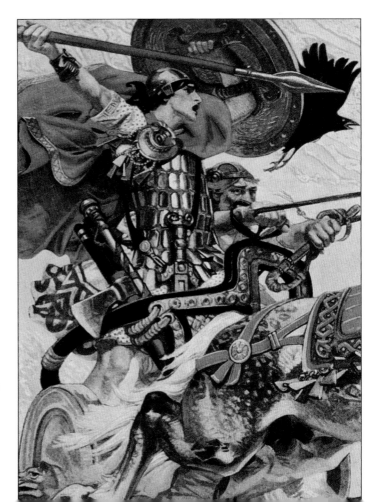

BELOW: Cú Chulainn's charioteer features as a friend and sidekick in many of his tales. The hero's chariot sometimes acts as a plot device, taking him from one scene to another and occasionally making a timely rescue.

cursed the men of Ulster to feel what she was experiencing every time they were in danger.

With most of the men of Ulster thus out of action, Cú Chullain set about holding off the invading army. He killed hundreds over several days with his sling or by raiding their camp. The men of Connacht then came to a curious agreement with Cú Chullain. He would fight a duel with one of their warriors each day, and the men of Connacht would press on while the fighting continued. They would make camp for the day if Cú Chullain won, however.

Cú Chullain held up the Connacht host in this way for a while. During this time the Morrigan approached Cú Chullain.

BELOW: Fer Diad only agreed to fight Cú Chulainn after he was threatened with bardic satirization. His reputation would have been ruined had he not fought the duel. Instead, Cú Chulainn reluctantly killed him.

As she had done on other occasions, she combined the aspects of fertility and war by essentially offering herself to Cú Chullain. Had he accepted, the Morrigan might have assisted him but, spurned, she instead made a nuisance of herself. Distracting Cú Chullain, she caused him to be wounded as he fought a warrior named Loch. Cú Chullain won this fight using the gae bolg, but was too badly hurt to fight on. It took Cú Chullain three days to heal, during which time his place was taken by his father, Lugh Lamfada.

During Cú Chullain's series of duels, one of the men sent against him was Fer Diad Mac Damann, Cú Chullain's boyhood friend and blood brother. Having refused various inducements to fight Cú Chullain, Fer Diad was eventually threatened with satirization by every bard in the land, and had no choice but to fight. The heroes battled for two days, but at the end of each they camped together and slept under the same blanket. They did not camp together at the end of the third day, and on the fourth Cú Chullain was forced to kill his friend with a cast of his gae bolg. Again Cú Chullain was grievously injured.

'HE KILLED HUNDREDS OVER SEVERAL DAYS WITH HIS SLING OR BY RAIDING THEIR CAMP.'

By the time Cú Chullain was fit to fight again, the brown bull had been captured and the army of Connacht was returning home. With the men of Ulster still incapacitated, a force of boys who were not old enough to be affected by the curse (like Cú Chullain) went against the men of Connacht and were massacred. This sent Cú Chullain into a rage, causing him to slay 70 of the enemy, but he couldn't stop Ulster from being plundered.

The warriors of Ulster finally recovered from the curse and pursued the army of Connacht. Cú Chullain defeated Queen Medb but spared her life. Meanwhile the two great bulls fought and the white-horned bull of Connacht was killed. The brown bull of Cooley lived long enough to return home before he, too, died.

Like many heroic sagas, the tale of Cú Chullain is filled with tragedy. His affair with Aife led to the birth of a son named Connla, but the child was under a geis or magical compulsion. He could not reveal his name nor refuse combat. Cú Chullain had given Aife a ring, and told her that once the boy was old enough to wear it he must be sent to Cú Chullain in Ireland. In due course the child arrived.

Although Connla was only seven years old, Cú Chullain somehow perceived him as a threat and demanded to know who he was. Connla could not answer, and could not refuse to fight Cú Chullain who slew his son with a cast of gae bolg. It was similarly a geis that doomed Cú Chullain. He was under a geis not to eat dog meat and another never to refuse hospitality. This allowed his enemies to trick him into breaking the first geis, thus ensuring his defeat.

This defeat came at the hands of Queen Medb and the families of men slain by Cú Chullain during his battles and

ABOVE: Queen Medb not only instigated the Cattle Raid of Cooley for spurious reasons, she also murdered her own sister. Years later, her sister's son took vengeance when he killed her with a piece of cheese launched from a sling.

adventures. In some versions, Cú Chullain was taunted by satirists into throwing his spear at them, and each time it was hurled back; in others, magical spears were made to slay kings. The first slew Cú Chullain's charioteer, the greatest of his peers, and the second his horse, the finest of its kind. With these two 'kings' down, the next cast struck Cú Chullain and mortally wounded him.

Whether he was wounded by the 30 barbs of his own gae bolg or by a spear made by others, Cú Chullain knew that he was dying. His belly was torn open by the spear, so he used his own intestines to tie himself to a rock so that he could die on his feet like a warrior. Even though she was his enemy, The Morrigan came to Cú Chullain in his last moments, perching on his shoulder in the form of a raven. This showed his enemies that he was still alive, and it was not until she flew away from his dead body that they dared approach him.

Fionn Mac Cumhaill

The great hero of the Fenian Cycle was Fionn Mac Cumhaill. The Fenian Cycle generally takes place in a less turbulent and violent era of Irish mythological history, although this is only a relative thing; Fionn Mac Cumhaill's father was killed in a power struggle and the infant Fionn only just escaped.

Fionn Mac Cumhaill was a descendent of Nuada of the Silver Hand, and was connected with other members of the Tuatha Dé Danann. His hunting dogs were the children of a Danann woman who had been turned into a dog, and thus were actually related to him. Although the hounds' mother returned to human form the children did not, but they were very intelligent and resourceful.

Clearly destined for greatness from the start, Fionn Mac Cumhaill became clan chieftain by means of a series of heroic tests. Along the way he gained his magic banner and sword, and also a bag containing the letters of the alphabet. The latter is significant as it connects Fionn Mac Cumhaill with the bardic traditions and the invention of literacy. Fionn Mac Cumhaill also gained wisdom when he helped the bard Finn Eces catch and cook the Salmon of Wisdom and accidentally ate some of it.

Fionn encountered the surviving warriors of his father's Fianna – the word means a band of warriors but came to refer specifically to Fionn Mac Cumhaill's group. He earned his right to lead the Fianna by defeating a supernatural enemy named Aillén. Aillén was one of the faerie folk, a member of the Tuatha Dé Danann, who brought terror each Samhain to Tara, seat of the High King of Ireland.

Aillén used magical music to put the defenders to sleep then burned Tara with his fiery breath. Fionn Mac Cumhaill knew he could only prevent this if he could resist the effects of the music, so he inhaled poison from his spear. This enabled him to kill Aillén and for this he was proclaimed leader of the Fianna.

Fionn Mac Cumhaill's adventures often revolved around romantic decisions. His affair with the wife of the King of France triggered an invasion of Ireland that was only barely prevented at the Battle of Ventry Bay. As the invasion force landed, Fionn Mac Cumhaill summoned every fighting-man in Ireland to resist, resulting in a battle that lasted a year and a day. The king of Ulster's son was driven mad by the conflict, and defeat seemed likely until aid arrived from the Tuatha dé Danann, whose warriors helped drive out the invaders.

BELOW: **Fionn's defeat of the faerie Aillén earned him the right to lead the Fianna, or warband, that protected the High King of Ireland. According to some accounts, Fionn and his Fianna now sleep in a cave, awaiting the hour of Ireland's greatest need.**

Fionn Mac Cumhaill was a vengeful man at times, especially as he grew older. After the death of his wife Maigneis, he sought a new companion and invited Gráinne, daughter of the Irish High King, to his court. Gráinne was reputedly the most beautiful woman in Ireland, and seems also to have had magical powers. She did not find the elderly Fionn Mac Cumhaill attractive, but preferred one of his warriors, Diarmuid. At first Diarmuid refused to betray his lord, but Gráinne used a geis to persuade him. Diarmuid and Gráinne escaped from Fionn Mac Cumhaill's stronghold and evaded his attempts to find them for some time. This was not least due to the assistance of Diarmuid's foster-father, Oengus Óg, a god of love who possessed a cloak of invisibility.

Eventually Fionn Mac Cumhaill found the lovers but agreed to put aside the quarrel when Oengus Óg intervened. However, he never forgave Diarmuid. When the warrior was injured during a boar hunt, Fionn Mac Cumhaill went to get healing waters for him but kept dropping them on the way back, therefore allowing Diarmuid to die of his injuries. This tale has many parallels with the Arthurian tragedy of Tristan and Iseult, which may indicate common origins or direct derivation.

The Death of Fionn Mac Cumhaill

Fionn Mac Cumhaill's death is the subject of several contradictory tales. In some, he does not die at all but sleeps in a hidden place, ready to return one day. Here is another parallel with some versions of the romance of King Arthur. However, most tales have Fionn Mac Cumhaill meeting his end in a violent manner. As with other Irish heroes the geis plays a part. Fionn Mac Cumhaill was forbidden to drink from a horn by a geis, and unwisely did so shortly before attempting to leap across the River Boyne. In this tale, Fionn Mac Cumhaill fell and struck his head during the attempt and died from his injuries.

Other versions of the tale have men rather than rocks as the cause of the hero's demise. As Fionn Mac Cumhaill and his Fianna grew in power, others plotted against them. Among them was Caibre, who wanted to be High King of Ireland. Fionn Mac Cumhaill, showing his characteristic poor judgment and lack of regard for others' sensibilities, demanded a large tribute or the right to sleep with Caibre's daughter in return for not blocking Caibre's plans.

The warriors of the Fianna included many heroes, as was fitting for such an illustrious group. More correctly named Fianna Éirann, the Fianna was an elite warband formed to protect the High King of Ireland. Its leader was so important and influential that he was at times referred to as a king. The Fianna was a political force as well as a military one; its leader had great political power. Not surprisingly perhaps, the position was coveted by man. However, traditionally only Clan Baiscne (Fionn Mac Cumhaill's clan) and Clan Morna were candidates for the leadership.

This naturally led to friction and at times conflict, such as the one that claimed the life of Fionn Mac Cumhaill's father. There was also division within the Fianna, not least because some of its members had fought against one another in the past. The former leader of the Fianna, Aed, changed his name to Goll (meaning one-eyed) after losing one of his eyes battling Cumhaill. He led the Fianna and enjoyed its power until challenged for leadership

BELOW: Poball Fhinn (Finn's People) is one of several stone circles on the Isle of North Uist in the Outer Hebrides. The stones are thought to be named for Fionn Mac Cumhaill. They were erected some 3000– 4000 years ago.

ABOVE: Oisín was a son of Fionn Mac Cumhaill and a member of the Fianna. As the greatest Bard in Ireland, he had many adventures including this journey to Tir na nÓg, the 'land of eternal youth in the Underworld.

by Cumhaill's son Fionn Mac Cumhaill. Afterward he resented his subordinate role and sided with the High King Caibre against the Fianna.

Caibre considered the Fianna too powerful – and perhaps Fionn Mac Cumhaill too full of himself to tolerate – so he joined forces with other Irish leaders. Together they made war on the Fianna, forcing them to fight a battle at Gabhra while heavily outnumbered. Caibre was killed by Oscar, Fionn's grandson and one of the greatest warriors of the Fianna, but Oscar was mortally wounded in the encounter.

The Fianna was defeated, although at heavy cost to both sides. Fionn Mac Cumhaill was either killed in this battle at Ath Brea or ambushed at Gabhra depending on the version. Either way, the power of the Fianna was broken and Fionn Mac Cumhaill was slain.

Few warriors survived the battle, and of them Oisín and Caílte were the most notable. According to some versions of the tale they journeyed to Tir na nÓg, land of eternal youth, and stayed there for a while. They returned to Ireland to find that 300 years had passed, and encountered Saint Patrick who recorded the deeds of Fionn Mac Cumhaill and his men. In this way the myths of pagan Ireland were incorporated into Christian histories.

Stories of Magic

There are numerous versions of the great Celtic tales, possibly because of the time period involved. It is possible that the story of a Pictish hero eventually became the tragic tale of Sir Tristan, which somehow became part of the Arthurian legends, although there was probably no original connection. Indeed, the tales of King Arthur are largely derived from Celtic legends originating in the British Isles and the Continent.

Many versions have emerged; in some Arthur dies and in others he journeys to the magical land of Avalon to await the time when he will be needed again. These conflicting versions of the tales are further confused by later reinterpretations and the incorporation of tales from other cultures. The legends of King Arthur lie somewhat outside the ancient Celtic myths yet are heavily influenced by them, much as later society adopted many Celtic concepts.

The Arthurian legends of Britain owe much to the collection of Welsh stories knows as the Mabinogion. Arthur plays a role in some of these tales, although they also feature the adventures of other Welsh heroes. The tale of Taliesin, which was not originally part of the Mabinogion but came from other sources, has a number of parallels with stories from other cultures. Taliesin was conceived when the sorceress Ceridwen swallowed Gwyon Bach. The latter had gained vast knowledge from accidentally consuming a magical brew that Ceridwen was preparing, wrecking the project in the process.

Gwyon Bach used his new knowledge to try to escape Ceridwen but ultimately failed despite repeatedly changing his shape. Ceridwen did likewise, and in the form of a hen ate Gwyon Bach while he was hiding among a pile of grain. Even in the form of grain, Gwyon Bach's power was considerable and caused Ceridwen to become pregnant. When the child was born he was so beautiful that Ceridwen decided not to kill him as she had intended, but instead mercifully tied him into a bag and threw him in the sea.

The infant floated for nine days before being caught by

BELOW: **The Arthurian tragedy of Tristan and Iseult may have been derived from an earlier tale in which Fionn Mac Cumhaill essentially murdered his friend Diarmuid for stealing the affections of Gráinne, daughter of the High King of Ireland.**

Elffin, nephew of the King of Wales, who was out fishing. His disappointment at catching a nine-day-old infant presumably turned to great surprise when the baby sang him a poem of consolation and recounted his adventures. He announced that he was the reincarnation of Gwyon Bach, but Elffin named him Taliesin and adopted him as foster-son.

Taliesin brought good luck to Elffin's household, and rescued his foster-father from a predicament caused by drunken boasting. Elffin had angered his uncle Maelgwn Gwynedd, the Welsh king and was imprisoned, so Taliesin saved him by proving that all of his foster father's boasts were actually true. He used his magic and wisdom to show that Elffin's wife was in fact more beautiful and virtuous than the queen, and that Elffin's horse was in fact faster than the king's. He struck the king's bards dumb with a spell, although their chief was able to determine the origin of the magic.

Taliesin then declared that he was the chief of all bards of the west, that he could control the weather and that this was his latest reincarnation in a line going back to the Creation. He proved all this with magic and tales, and ultimately King

BELOW: **King Bran the Blessed led an ill-fated expedition to Ireland to save his sister Branwen from mistreatment. Only seven men survived the battles and treachery that resulted. Since Bran's body was too large to bring home, they bore his severed head back with them.**

Maelgwn Gwynedd could only accept it as true. He was thus forced to accept that Elffin had spoken truly, and released him.

Taliesin is an ambiguous figure, perhaps a man with supernatural powers and wisdom or possibly a demi-god. Many of the other figures in Welsh Celtic mythology are mortals who have dealings with otherworldly powers. The chieftain Pwyll ran afoul of Arawn, King of Annwvyn. Annwvyn was the Otherworld, the Welsh equivalent of the Irish Sidhe. In amends for the offence he had given Pwyll was to swap places with Arawn for a year.

Annwvyn had another king, Havgan, and Arawn's plan was for Pwyll to defeat him. During his year-long stint as King of the Otherworld, Pwyll did so, severely wounding Havgan but sparing his life. What he did not do was have sex with Arawn's wife, even though they slept in the same bed for a year and she (like everyone else in the Otherworld) did not know he was an impostor. This won Arawn's friendship and favour, and Pwyll was rewarded richly. He returned to his own domain to find it greatly improved by Arawn's stewardship.

> 'HE SENT BRANWEN TO WORK IN THE KITCHENS, AND CONCEALED HIS TREATMENT OF HER.'

King Bran the Blessed

Other Welsh heroes had unusual powers. King Bran the Blessed was a giant who had a beautiful sister named Branwen. Bran received Mallolwch, King of Ireland, at his court, and agreed to allow Branwen to marry Mallolwch. However, an incident at court led Bran needing to make amends to the Irish king. He gifted Mallolwch with fine horses and a magical cauldron that could bring the dead back to life.

Mallolwch was at first happy with his bride, but eventually was convinced that the Welsh King Bran should have made greater gifts in recompense. He sent Branwen to work in the kitchens, and concealed his treatment of her from outsiders. Branwen trained a starling to deliver a message to her brother, who decided to make war upon Ireland.

Bran's men travelled by ship, but he was tall enough to wade across the sea to Ireland. His size was also beneficial during the campaign that followed. Bran lay across the river Liffey to replace the bridge that Mallolwch had demolished, and Mallolwch realized that he could not simply retreat. Instead he offered a peace settlement that disguised a trap, luring Bran into a house where 200 men were hidden in bags that he claimed were filled with flour.

Bran's half-brother Evnissyen squeezed the bags, killing the ambushers, so Mallolwch decided to honour his suggested peace settlement as if he had meant to all along. This went about as well as might be expected, and soon Bran's men were fighting those of King Mallolwch. Bran's gift of the magical cauldron proved his undoing, as the Irish were able to bring their warriors back to life – including the 200 already disposed of – faster than Bran's men could kill them. The battle turned when Evnissyen, who had caused the initial incident and the breakdown of the peace process, had himself been placed alive into the magical cauldron. This undid its magic and caused it to shatter, as only the dead were supposed to be placed in it. Evnissyen died, but the endless supply of reinforcements was cut off and Bran's men won the battle… more or less.

All of the Irish were slain, and only seven Welshmen survived including the bard Taliesin. Bran was killed by a poisoned spear and died soon after, and Branwen died of a broken heart a little later. Bran's body was too large to carry home, so the seven survivors honoured his last wish by taking his head back to Wales. Along the way they tarried for 80 years in a magical hall in Gwales. There they forgot about their grief and were happy until a certain door was opened and they remembered what had happened. The seven then left the hall and buried Bran's head in London.

One of the survivors of the expedition was Manawyddan, Bran's brother. He had no kingdom to return to, as his cousin had usurped the throne during the long years of absence. Manawyddan was offered new lands by Pryderi, son of the chieftain Pwyll. Manawyddan married Pryderi's mother Rhiannon (who was at the time a widow) and lived with Pryderi and his wife Kigva.

Misfortune struck when all of the people in Dyved, Pryderi's kingdom, mysteriously vanished leaving just the four members of Pryderi's household. With the kingdom empty of people they were forced to move elsewhere and try to make a living as tradesmen. The problem was that Pryderi and Manawyddan were simply too good at everything they did, and were driven off by mobs of angry lesser craftsmen wherever they tried to settle.

The four eventually went back to Dyved, but the people were still missing. Pryderi and then Rhiannon disappeared. Manawyddan and Kigva returned to England and tried farming, but their crop was eaten by mice. Manawyddan caught one of the mice and naturally decided to hang it as a thief. A succession of people tried to dissuade him, but Manawyddan was adamant until a visiting archbishop asked what he wanted in return for sparing the mouse. Manawyddan said he would only accept the return of Rhiannon and Pryderi, plus the missing population of Dyved.

ABOVE: Rhiannon, mother of Pryderi, came to the notice of her first husband Pwyll as she rode by. Although her horse moved slowly, no-one on foot or horseback could catch up until Pwyll cleverly thought of calling out to her to stop.

Llywd's Revenge

The archbishop turned out to be Llywd, whose friend Gwawl had feuded with Pwyll and decided to take revenge upon his son Pryderi. Llywd had turned his followers into mice to attack Manawyddan's crops, and the mouse that got caught was none other than Llywd's wife. Manawyddan agreed to return her if Llywd ended the spells on Dyved and vowed not to resume the quarrel. This was done and the four went home to Dyved to find the people had also returned.

Pryderi met his end in battle with Math, son of Mathonwy and lord of Gwynedd, as the result of a plot by others. For reasons that remain obscure Math liked to rest his feet in the lap of a virgin. The virgin in question, Goewin, was desired by Math's nephew Gilvaethwy. In order to get his uncle out of the way, Gilvaethwy and his brother Gwydyon created a conflict with Pryderi's realm.

The brothers used trickery to obtain from Pryderi some pigs given to his father Pwyll by Arawn, King of the Otherworld. When the gifts given in return for the pigs turned out to be illusions, Pryderi pursued the brothers, who told their uncle that Dyved was marching on Gwynedd. Math led his army out and defeated Pryderi in the field. Pryderi challenged Math and was killed in single combat.

While Math led his forces to meet the attack, Gilvaethwy took the opportunity to rape Goewin. Math punished the brothers by turning them into male and female animals – first deer then boar then wolves. Each time the brothers were forced to mate in animal form and produced young, which Math turned back into humans. Meanwhile, now that he could no longer rest his feet in her lap, Math married Goewin.

BELOW: Blodeuedd's punishment for her betrayal of Lleu was to be turned into an owl. She would never dare go abroad in daylight again and would be hated by all other birds.

The Magical Baby

When Gwydyon's punishment was over, Math allowed him to return to court and advise on the selection of a new virgin. Gwydyon proposed his sister Aranhrod, but when Math used magic to see if she was genuinely a virgin, she immediately produced a child. This boy was named Dylan and was adopted by Math, but a second baby went unnoticed by everyone except Gwydyon who took him away and hid him.

The magical baby grew quickly, and Gwydyon eventually presented her to Aranhrod, who immediately cursed him three times. The first curse was that the boy – who had not yet been named even though he was four years old – would never have a name unless Aranhrod herself gave him one. The second curse was that he could not have armour or weapons until she gave them to him, and the third was that he could never have a wife.

Gwydyon tricked Aranhrod into naming and arming the baby by using magic to disguise him. Aranhrod named the child Lleu of the Skillful Hand and armed him while under the impression that a raiding fleet was nearing the coast. The third curse, however, proved to be more of a problem. Math solved this by creating a beautiful woman named Blodeuedd out of flowers with his magic.

'MATH PUNISHED THE BROTHERS BY TURNING THEM INTO MALE AND FEMALE ANIMALS.'

Unfortunately Blodeuedd fell in love with Goronwy the Staunch, a rival lord, and revealed to him the only way that Lleu could be killed. He must be attacked with a spear that took a year to make while standing with one foot on a goat and the other in water. Despite meeting these specific set of requirements, Goronwy failed to slay Lleu, who turned into an eagle and flew away.

Math sent Gwydyon to search for Lleu, and found him still in the form of an eagle, starving and weak. He turned Lleu back into human form and helped him recover, after which Lleu led a force against Goronwy and Blodeuedd. The latter fled but was caught by Gwydyon, who turned her into an owl. Goronwy tried to bargain for his life, and came to the agreement with Lleu that he would stand as Lleu had done and allow him to cast a spear, but that Goronwy would be allowed the protection of a rock between him and the spear.

Lleu agreed to this and threw the spear right through the rock, killing Goronwy. He thus regained his lands and later succeeded King Math. The parallels with the Irish Lugh, who was also known for his skills and ability to kill people with projectiles, are striking. Lugh was also a misplaced baby, one of three brothers who were to be killed but was somehow overlooked, and, like Lleu, Lugh came to rule the people of his land.

5

TECHNOLOGY AND WARFARE

The ancient Celts were highly adept at making effective tools and weapons. Bronze tools were among the key export items of the Hallstatt region until they were replaced by equally well-made iron items.

Metalworking was both robust and intricate, allowing beautiful goods to be made as well as high-quality workaday tools. This in turn meant that the Celts could undertake precision work when it was desirable.

This may seem at odds with the popular image of people who lived in squalid huts. Why would a culture that could twist gold wire into intricate designs choose to live in such crude dwellings? The answer of course is that the homes of the Celts were neither crude nor squalid. They were well made out of natural materials, robust and likely to withstand even British weather for many years without large amounts of maintenance. They were also warm and comfortable; in short, a Celtic home was a good place to live.

OPPOSITE: **The Gundestrup Cauldron is the largest piece of ancient European silverwork ever found by archaeologists. It dates from first or second century BCE and depicts Celtic images such as warriors and an antlered man or god.**

The most common Celtic dwelling in the British Isles was the round house, although in other areas rectangular buildings were used at times. A round house (or its equivalent) was constructed using vertical poles to support the roof and then filling in between the poles with walls made of wattle and daub. A steeply sloping thatched roof was highly effective at keeping rain and wind out.

'THE MOST COMMON CELTIC DWELLING IN THE BRITISH ISLES WAS THE ROUND HOUSE.'

Wattle and daub construction used vertical sticks as supports, with lighter twigs woven between them horizontally to create a framework. Hazel or willow were the preferred materials as the twigs had to be pliable enough not to snap when threaded between the supports. This framework was then covered with a mixture of straw, clay and animal dung that set hard to create a weatherproof wall. Many roundhouses were then whitewashed with lime.

One reason for whitewashing was aesthetic – white or off-white huts looked better than brown ones – but lightening the interior walls also reflected more light, making it easier to see.

BELOW: **Various designs of Celtic houses have been reconstructed, demonstrating highly sophisticated building techniques. The resulting dwelling is not a grand edifice but it does provide a comfortable, durable and secure home.**

It is easy to assume that round houses were dark, smoky places but this was not the case. In the author's experience, gained from visiting reconstructed Iron Age dwellings, the round house was a surprisingly pleasant, airy environment and not nearly as dark as might be expected.

In daytime, sufficient light entered the round house to see by and to conduct most tasks, and at night the fire, perhaps augmented by rush lights, provided some light. Most tasks were carried out by daylight, often outside, with the house being a place to sleep and to live rather than a workplace. Like most people, until the advent of strong artificial lighting the Celts rose with the dawn and made the most of the natural light.

LEFT: **Most work was done outside the round house, where the light was better. The interior was centred on a fire pit, which provided light as well as heat for cooking. The conical roof helped guide smoke out of the living area.**

Round houses were typically clustered together into a small village, which might or might not have some basic fortifications. If present, these generally took the form of a low earth rampart, often fronted with a ditch created when the rampart building materials were dug out. The rampart might be topped with a wooden palisade, usually formed of logs sharpened at the top. Some palisades were removable, giving the villagers better access to their settlement in peacetime but available to be emplaced if danger threatened.

Building Defences

Greater security was afforded by a hill-fort, which as the name suggests was constructed on high ground. Some hill-forts were completely surrounded by one or more rings of earthworks and ditches, and some used stone walls instead of or in addition to earthworks. Others enjoyed partial protection from steep slopes and difficult terrain, and these often had only partial fortifications covering the easiest avenues of approach for an enemy force.

ABOVE: **The first round house reconstructed at Castell Henleys in Wales was more than 20 years ago. Three others and a granary have since been rebuilt, all on their original Iron Age foundations, and others have been rebuilt at several sites.**

Although these partial forts may look primitive, they were effective in providing good defence, and perhaps more importantly they were cost-effective in terms of the effort invested. It is difficult to estimate how much any given investment of time and money into defences might be worth. For a tribe that was never attacked the effort would be entirely wasted, but such were the times that at least some conflict would be inevitable.

Celtic hill-forts were not designed to withstand an organized army equipped with siege engines. Some were attacked by such forces – usually Roman armies – and still provided reasonable protection, but they were never intended to resist such an organized force. The typical opponents faced by a Celtic tribe were other Celts, who had only the most basic of siege warfare techniques. Against them, an earth rampart or partially fortified hill was a real obstacle that could enable defenders to hold out or threaten the attackers with prohibitively high casualties.

Nor could the average Celtic tribe maintain a siege for long. Warriors were not professionals and had farms or businesses to get back to, and there was no real provision for long-term logistics. Tribal warfare was generally a matter of raids and short campaigns culminating in a skirmish or battle rather than an organized attempt to conquer and hold territory or subjugate people. In this context, retreating into a hill-fort was a viable tactic that would reduce losses, although the attackers were then able to plunder or destroy what they wanted.

It was not possible for a whole tribe to live in a hill-fort, and indeed some were not permanently inhabited at all. The fort was a refuge in times of danger and also a mustering point for the warriors of the tribe, who would then go out to attack their enemies or meet the invasion. The fort could act as a safe haven for families during a conflict or a place to retreat to if the conflict was not going well.

Conflict was common in the Celtic world, but for the most part it took the form of inter-tribal raiding and bickering rather than conquest, subjugation or annihilation. This constant low-level fighting, with occasional large-scale conflicts, produced formidable warriors. Celtic fighting-men were, man for man, as good as or better than the legionaries of Rome or any other professional force. However, the same conflicts that made Celts good at fighting rendered them rather less effective at waging war.

Celtic Warfare

Raids for plunder and glory, or to chastise the enemies of the tribe for some real or imagined wrong, could be carried out by small bands of fairly disorganized – but certainly enthusiastic – part-time warriors. A war of conquest might be fought against a similar foe by such forces, resulting in surrender and subjugation, but there was a limit to how much the Celts could achieve in warfare.

BELOW: Fortified homesteads have existed throughout history. A walled enclosure protects the dwellings as well as various outbuildings such as cattle sheds and granaries. Many Celtic farmsteads were home to an extended family plus some unrelated workers, possibly with families of their own.

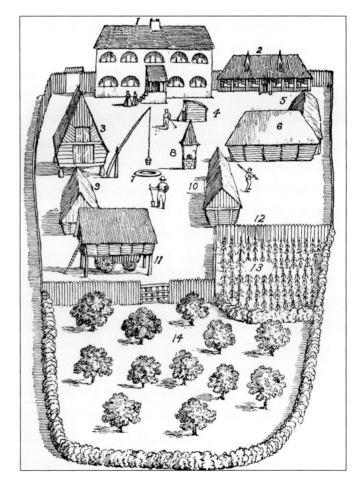

These limits arose mainly from two causes. The first was the inability of the Celts to unite for long. A charismatic leader or a very dire emergency might cause several tribes to work together for a time, but even then there would be disagreements and possibly even conflict among the supposed allies. Command and control would be a nightmare, with proud leaders unwilling to subordinate themselves to anyone, and bickering over precedence at a time when unity was vital.

The second reason was the lack of a formal military structure. Information and orders were not passed according to a well-understood and coherent system, and as a result leaders had at best patchy information from scouts. They might not know where some of their allies were, nor what they intended or even if they were willing to fight. Orders might not get to those that were supposed to receive them, and they could be refused even if they did. Indeed, a leader might take umbrage at being given an order and enter into a conflict against his supposed commander.

These weaknesses were not a major problem when the Celts warred among themselves or against similar opponents, and indeed the nature of the Celtic military system – such as it was – helped preserve a balance between tribes and ensure that while some were diminished or displaced, eradication was unlikely and the balance of power remained more or less the same. This may well have contributed to the longevity of the Celtic way of life; constant low-level conflict relieved pressure but did not cause enormous upheavals.

Against more formally organized opponents, however, the deficiencies in the Celtic military system were very apparent. During Julius Caesar's Gallic campaigns, the Battle of Alesia is recorded as pitting Caesar's 70,000 Romans against a slightly

BELOW: **Roman observers referred to fortified Celtic settlements, especially those that were an administrative centre, as Oppida. The Oppidum (hill-fort) at Citania de Briteiros was originally a Celtiberian stronghold. It shows some Roman influence, though it fell into disuse after the Roman conquest of Iberia.**

superior force within the city, and also having to beat off attacks from as many as 250,000 more Gauls in the relief army. This version of history probably included a very large element of self-acclamatory exaggeration, with the odds against Caesar greatly overstated by his biographer (who was none other than Caesar himself!) for the purposes of propaganda.

Even if these vast numbers of warriors were raised by the Gauls, they could not be supported in the field for long, nor could they be wielded with any sort of effectiveness. Far from being an unstoppable steamroller under the hand of the Celtic leaders, the army was a vast unwieldy mass that was prone to fragment at the most inopportune times.

It may have been that 250,000 or more Gauls were under arms and prepared to fight Rome, but there was no way to concentrate them or to undertake rapid responses to a changing situation. Just supplying that many fighting men was an impossibility, forcing elements of the Celtic force to

ABOVE: **The Roman fortifications at Alesia were formidable, with ditches topped by a palisade and covered by towers. Any assault on the Roman force had to struggle up a steep slope, showered with pila, before coming to handstrokes.**

be detached in order to forage. Mistrust among the tribes and an unwillingness to take orders from rivals further divided the Gallic host, and this division was exploited by Romans to whom politics and warfare were more or less the same thing. If a tribe could be neutralized by economic or political means, or induced to fall out with its allies, then that was as useful as defeating its forces in the field; perhaps more so.

The Roman army, by contrast, was well organized and well supplied, with an efficient system to keep it fed and combat-ready and most importantly able to bring heavy fighting power to bear at the key point. If the Roman army could be compared to a surgeon's knife in its precise application of force, then the Celtic host was a large sponge. If the Gallic leaders cooperated at the right time they might be able to smother the Roman force, but it was far more likely their army would be cut to pieces by repeated strikes at critical points. Indeed, although the Romans might be vastly outnumbered in Gaul, their ability to react faster than their opponents meant that at times the Gauls had to fight outnumbered, with elements of their force too far off or otherwise unwilling or unable to join the battle.

For the ancient Celts, warfare was very much a personal matter. There were few, if any, professional warriors and nothing that could be called a formally trained soldier. A chieftain would lead a warband of the best warriors, and these men would become skilled as they gained experience, but their main occupation was not warfare. In a time of great conflict these men might see a lotof action, and at times most of the tribe would be under arms, which might create the impression of a professional warrior class. Celtic warriors went to fight because the tribe needed them to, their friends and neighbours expected it and their peers were willing to go as well. Some probably went out to fight because they liked it.

Leadership Style

Similarly, leadership was a personal matter. A charismatic chieftain or a skilled warrior would be able to get others to follow him, but this was a matter for individual choice and social pressure rather than a formal system with clearly defined duties and penalties for failing to uphold them. Celtic kings and chieftains led rather than commanded, getting stuck in alongside the rest of the warriors and showing the way by example.

One of the drawbacks of this system was the general clumsiness of Celtic field forces. Complex manoeuvres were not possible without a good command and control apparatus. Instead it was mainly a question of when to charge and who at, and once the attack was in motion then combat tended to be a fairly disorganized affair with individuals helping one another as best they could.

> 'A CHARISMATIC CHIEFTAIN OR A SKILLED WARRIOR WOULD BE ABLE TO GET OTHERS TO FOLLOW HIM.'

Some Celtic warriors and leaders did possess good tactical sense, and would direct their attacks at the weak point of an enemy force or shift the direction of an attack to exploit an advantage. This was generally on a small scale once the battle was joined, however. Thus while Brennus was able to concentrate his force's attack on the weak wings of the Roman army at the Battle of the River Allia, once the forces made contact it was mainly a matter of fighting it out until one side or the other gave way.

The Celts were good at this kind of close-quarters scrapping, and if they could get in among their foes then their individual fighting power was extremely potent. If the enemy force remained intact, however, then the Celtic charge could be repelled by a shield wall, a phalanx of spears or the massed volley of Roman pila followed by a countercharge. Superior discipline and organization held the key to defeating Celts – fighting them man-to-man was generally a recipe for disaster.

Although their warriors were fairly lightly equipped in terms of armour and protection, the Celts fought as a primarily heavy infantry force. Their tactics relied mainly on shock action and direct aggression to overwhelm their enemies. There was no concept of combined arms as such; archers were used as an expedient occasionally and thrown spears were incorporated into the general melee, but the idea of mutually supporting troop types was not one to which the Celts readily took.

BELOW: **The Celtic style of leadership was very personal, with a chieftain leading his men in person. If he set a good example, his force would probably fight well. However, his death or serious injury could demoralize his followers.**

When forced onto the defensive, Celtic forces generally used a shield wall formation. Formed by overlapping shields, the wall was a physically and psychologically resilient formation, although it rendered the Celtic force more or less immobile. A shield wall was hard for the enemy to break into, and anyone who tried had to come into range of the warriors' weaponry, but in order to attack or escape from a disastrously bad situation the shield wall had to break up.

The impulsive nature of Celtic warriors was such that a shield wall could be broken by accident, such as by an enemy who suffered a bad repulse and fell back but was not defeated. As some of the Celts came out of their defensive formation to press their perceived advantage, they became vulnerable to renewed attack. Conversely, a shield wall was a way of avoiding defeat but to win the Celts had to advance out of their formation. Organizing this was problematic.

Each leader, and indeed possibly every warrior within the shield wall, would have his own ideas about exactly when the moment was right to charge out of the shield wall and attack a wavering enemy. If the counterattack was ill-timed the Celtic force risked either letting an enemy retire undefeated or rushing headlong to destruction. Post-battle bickering was inevitable if some wanted to attack and others thought that the time was not right.

Chariot Warriors

Celtic forces also made use of chariots, although these had fallen out of favour elsewhere and been largely replaced by cavalry. The Celtic chariot was a status symbol as much as a weapon or vehicle; numerous chariot burials have been discovered. Many of the heroes of Celtic mythology were famous for their chariot use, and they were useful weapons when deployed correctly.

The Celtic chariot was a light, two-man vehicle drawn by a pair of horses. The central driving platform was slung using a form of suspension rather than being directly fixed to the axle, which created a more stable fighting platform. The warrior stood here, with the driver seated in front of him and fully occupied by driving the chariot.

According to some sources, in some tribes the chariot driver was a man of high station, who conveyed one or more warriors to the battlefield and sent them off to fight. This is at odds with the Celtic concept of personal heroism, but there were many tribes so differing conventions are possible. It was more common for the charioteer to be a social inferior, serving a high-status warrior or leader. A good charioteer was well respected but was very much a part of the hero's team as a sidekick rather than being a hero in his own right.

The chariot forces would open a battle by dashing aggressively upon the enemy, creating a profound psychological shock that could unnerve some foes. The warriors would hurl spears from their chariots before swerving away, leaving the enemy unable to come to contact. This harassment went on for a while before

ABOVE: **The large Celtic shield was formed of wood typically with a cloth or leather covering. It gave good protection to an individual, and allowed a force to create an instant fortification by overlapping their shields into a wall.**

RIGHT: There are a few accounts of the Celts using scythed chariots, but no real evidence that they did so. This rather crude and clumsy vehicle would not be well suited to the highly mobile style of warfare that Celtic charioteers practised.

the main assault took place. At this point the warriors would leap from their chariots and charge the enemy. Their charioteers would withdraw to a safe distance and remain ready to rush up and rescue their warriors if they got into serious trouble.

This ability to act as skirmishing cavalry, then to deploy an infantry force very close to the enemy line, made chariots highly effective in Celtic hands. There are accounts of warriors running up the chariot yoke to take a better shot at the enemy, and leaping in and out of chariots at speed. This not only made Celtic chariot forces hard to pin down and defeat but caused a great deal of confusion and dismay at this highly unconventional kind of fighting. The ability to pick up wounded or beleaguered warriors and retire at great speed enabled Celtic chariots to harass superior enemy forces yet avoid being decisively defeated.

Although various claims have been made – often by Roman commentators – that the Celts of the British Isles used chariots with scythe-like blades attached to the wheels, this is unlikely. There is no archaeological evidence for scythed chariots, and while some writers mention them, most do not. Indeed, the mode of use described by Roman writers is not consistent with scythed chariots – the Celts used them as transport, not projectiles to be sent into enemy ranks. Such scythed-chariot charges are one-shot affairs, and would preclude using the vehicles to retire from the battlefield, which the Celts are explicitly recorded as doing.

However, there are numerous references to spikes and other projections on the chariots of Celtic heroes, so perhaps there was limited use of such devices in at least some areas.

Fighting with Spears

Like many similar cultures, the Celts made extensive use of spears in warfare. A spear is a fairly simple weapon to make, requiring only a shaped wooden shaft and a small amount of metal that need not be of especially high quality or workmanship. A spear point does not need to bear the same stresses as the long blade of a sword and can be quite crudely cast and still be effective. Although the Celts were excellent metalsmiths, simple weapons still represented a good tradeoff in terms of time invested to fighting power. A spear gave the Celtic warrior an extended reach in combat, ideally allowing him to disable his enemy without risking a blow in return.

At the same time, a spear is a more flexible weapon than many people realize. It would normally be used with a shield, but a skilled spearman could take his weapon in both hands and use it as a combination of staff and spear, 'choking up' the weapon to fight at close quarters and extending again as needed. A stout spear shaft could block many blows, although its primary defensive advantage was the ability to make enemies keep their distance.

The head of a spear was often sharpened on the sides, allowing opportunistic slashing blows. These were not as lethal as a direct thrust, but a warrior who missed a thrust could lay his spearhead on his opponent's flesh and draw it back towards him, causing a possibly disabling cut, or could make short sideways slashes at the face or limbs. Such a cut might not stop a determined warrior, but someone who found himself bleeding might consider it wise to retire from the fight, or might be weakened or distracted enough for a finishing thrust.

Spear designs varied according to purpose and preference. The thrusting spear or lancea was typically about 1.8m (5ft 10in) in length, or about the height of a typical Celtic man.

BELOW: The Celtic spear had a broad head that was sharpened on both sides, allowing the wielder to make opportunistic cuts as well as the more usual thrusts. It was the primary Celtic missile weapon.

The gaesum, or throwing spear, was somewhat shorter. Warriors might carry several throwing spears, hurling them at the enemy before closing for hand-to-hand combat. Some of the younger warriors, who were not yet fully-grown and capable of wielding a sword in battle, would fight as javelinmen, darting about throwing spears at any suitable target while avoiding contact with heavily armed opponents.

Sometimes other missile weapons were used, notably the sling. Slings are mentioned in both myths and historical writings as being common weapons, often used in defence of hill-forts. Slingstones were collected rather than formed from metal, with well-rounded pebbles from the beds of streams being favoured. This may have been more than expediency; the Celts generally revered bodies of water and the slingstones given to a warrior by a river may have had fortunate connotations.

'THE LONG SLASHING SWORD COULD STRIKE HARD FROM A REASONABLE DISTANCE.'

Bows were also used at times, although references to them are rare. It is recorded that the Gauls made extensive use of the bow while besieged at Alesia, which might have been expedient deployment of what was normally considered only a hunting weapon. Archeological finds suggest that bows were used in defensive fighting, but the evidence suggests that they were not a favoured battlefield weapon and that the Celts did not field forces of specialist archers. This would run contrary to the up-close-and-personal style of Celtic warfare and their heroic ideals of warriorhood.

However, skill at spear-throwing and slinging stones was considered worthy of heroes. There are numerous tales of heroes who defeat their enemies with a clever shot. Throwing a spear – and, to a somewhat lesser extent, using a sling – required the warrior to be quite close to his enemy and exposed to return fire or perhaps a charge. Spear-throwing was to a great extent still part of hand-to-hand combat, whereas shooting a bow could be seen as something a little different and less glorious.

The spear was often backed up by a sidearm. For poorer men this was a simple knife, which could be used for close-quarters combat if the spear was lost. More affluent warriors favoured the sword as a personal weapon. The original weapons were short, more or less overgrown knives and were used for stabbing. As metallurgy improved, a longer slashing sword, with a characteristic leaf-shaped blade, began to appear. This weapon was well suited to the individualistic style of Celtic combat, as it required a certain amount of space to use effectively.

The Cut and Thrust of the Sword

The long slashing sword could strike hard from a reasonable distance. Its wielder had about as much reach as someone using a spear in one hand, unless the spearman made a heavily committed, extended thrust. The arc of the sword also endangered an opponent within reach, as opposed to the spear thrust that was only dangerous along a very narrow path. Thus a swinging sword (or the threat of a swing) actually gave the warrior a measure of defence.

The sword was effective against the limbs and head, which were not easy targets for a thrusting spear, but it could also cut deep into the torso. A spear wound to the body would be more likely to kill an opponent, but a slash across the arm or leg might well put him out of the fight just as effectively, or could open him up for a killing blow. A slash could generally be delivered with less risk than a committed thrust.

The sword could also be used defensively if the shield was lost or unavailable, but the Celts did not fence with their opponents. Their style of combat was an aggressive attack. The Celtic method of fighting influenced others in many ways. Notably, Roman protective equipment was designed to defend against an overhead blow with a sword such as that favoured by the Gauls. With the head and shoulders well protected against the most likely attack, the Roman soldier was trained to thrust his short sword under the arm or into the chest cavity of an attacking Gaul.

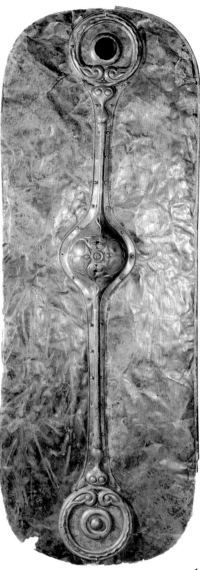

ABOVE: **This bronze-faced shield was recovered from the River Witham in Lincolnshire. It was decorated in a manner common in the La Tène period. General design follows the 'Gaulish' style, which was common to much of the Celtic world.**

Ironically perhaps, the iconic Roman sword was invented by the Celtiberians. Rather than a long slashing weapon, the Gladius Hispaniensis ('Spanish Sword') had a fairly short blade and was primarily used for stabbing, although it could deliver a powerful cut. The Roman weapon was well suited to use by disciplined soldiers rather than would-be heroes, and proved an effective counter to the common style of aggressive Celtic swordsmanship.

The Celtic sword, like the Roman, was primarily used with a shield. Designs varied, although a generally oval or rectangular shape was favoured. Round or even hexagonal shields have been found in Celtic burial sites, as well as shields that were clearly ceremonial as opposed to being intended for battle. Both combat and ceremonial shields were often highly decorated, although a battle shield might well be badly damaged in a fight and was less likely to carry lavish decoration.

Body Protection

The shield was formed from wood, with a central boss to protect the user's hand and to provide a place to mount a grip. Shields often had metal reinforcement and were usually faced with leather or cloth to prevent the wood from splitting. This still occurred of course – a powerful blow could smash a shield and render it useless. However, the shield was not designed to act as a simple wall to hide behind. Fighting with sword and shield (or spear and shield) was a complex art that had a lot more to it than attacking with the weapon and placing the shield in the way of a blow.

A skilled fighter used his shield as a weapon as well as defensively. He could push it out to block an enemy's vision of what he was doing, or jam it against his opponent's weapon arm in what is commonly called a 'shield bind'. The shield could be angled to deflect a blow or pushed out to intercept it at a point where it was weak. Shields also provided a measure of defence against arrows and other missiles.

Getting past the shield was part of the warrior's art. It was of course possible to cut or thrust over or under the shield at legs or the head, or to simply smash away at it in the hope of breaking it. Skilled warriors had other methods, however, such as stamping on the lower part of an enemy's shield to drive it down into the ground and send the user off balance. A warrior had to be alert for attacks against his shield as well as against his body.

The shield was not the only protection used by some warriors. Most owned no armour and fought in whatever clothes they normally wore, typically trousers, shirt and cloak, but some may have fought bare-chested or even naked. If so, the reasoning behind the latter was either religious – emulating supernatural heroes who were said to have fought without clothing – or perhaps psychological.

An enemy who fought naked, perhaps adorned with tattoos or whose skin was dyed blue with woad, could be intimidating. It is possible that some Celtic warriors sought to frighten their enemies with nakedness, projecting a complete disregard for their own safety by eschewing any form of protection. It is equally possible that they believed that fighting naked would invite supernatural protection. If Celtic warriors really did fight naked, there was probably a good reason for it – but the reason might have varied from one group to another.

Those that could afford armour wore it. A torc of bronze or gold around the neck might ward off a blow if the wearer was very lucky, and was augmented in many cases by a helmet and jerkin of leather. Richer warriors used metal armour, either in the form of reinforcement on a leather base or as the main component in their armour.

The Celts invented chain mail, a shirt of interlocking metal rings on a padded or leather backing that spread out the impact of a weapon and prevented a sharp point or edge from penetrating. Chain mail was very time-consuming and therefore expensive to make, requiring that metal wire be made and then formed into rings,

BELOW: **It is possible that many Celtic warriors went into action bare-chested but wearing brightly decorated trousers, and were subsequently described as naked either mistakenly or as a reference to their lack of armour.**

after which the laborious process of assembling the garment and riveting the rings together could begin. Such protection was only affordable by the richest of warriors, and marked the wearer as someone of great import.

Psychological Warfare

The ancient Celts were well aware of the psychological element in warfare. The noisy chariot charge and the (possible) practice of charging into action naked would unnerve enemies, but these were not the only psychological gambits used by the Celts. Noise, in the form of chanting and cheering, clashing weapons and blowing horns, was also used to good effect. Indeed, Gaius Marius felt the need to inure his Roman troops to the sights, sounds and smells of their barbarian opponents before venturing out to fight and ultimately defeat them at the Battle of Aquae Sextiae.

The concept of using tall helmets or fitting head protection with crests, horns or other decoration to make the warrior look taller and more fearsome has been used by many cultures, but the Celts took it to an unusual extreme at times. One of the most notable Celtic archeological finds was a helmet with a model of a raven atop it. This was designed so that the wings would flap when the wearer was in motion. Not only might this be distracting to an opponent, it also carried a powerful symbology – ravens were associated with death, so the wearer was seen as bringing death with him to the battlefield.

If time before a battle permitted, Celtic leaders were prone to approach the enemy lines and taunt their opponents or issue challenges to single combat. If refused, this made the enemy commanders look weak and fearful, and if accepted there was a good chance of depriving the enemy of key

BELOW: Many different helmet designs were used by the Celts, with and without ear and neck protection. Some designs had crests or other decoration intended to make the wearer seem larger and more intimidating to his foes.

personnel. Celtic warriors would also tell stories of their own and their ancestors' victories and boast of what they had done – and what they were about to do – to raise the morale of their own side.

The ancient Celts saw heads as having great spiritual significance. Taking the heads of defeated enemies was a way to gain power and prestige. A severed head could be displayed hanging at a warrior's belt or from his horse or chariot. Previous victims might be displayed at the warrior's house, which would gain him a reputation as a fearsome fighter and someone not to be opposed among his own people.

Much of the psychological element of warfare went on before the battle, in the form of creating a culture in which warriors were expected to perform heroic deeds. A Celt's worth was measured in terms of what others thought of him so it was not surprising that when they fought these people were ferocious indeed. Their cultural heroes included men who would tie themselves to a rock with their own intestines so as to die proud and upright, and heroes who could take on hordes of enemies and win.

The typical Celtic warrior went into action with high expectations on him. The deeds of his peers and ancestors, the pride of his tribe and the example of other warriors would inspire him and hopefully chase away the fear of battle. A Celt thrust into his first battle knew that he came from a proud and warlike culture, and if the Dagda's harp was capable of demolishing several Fomorian warriors then a man with a good sword or spear could surely vanquish whoever stood before him. These cultural psychological advantages are hard to quantify, but they certainly contributed to the effectiveness of the individual Celt in battle.

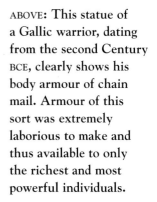

ABOVE: **This statue of a Gallic warrior, dating from the second Century BCE, clearly shows his body armour of chain mail. Armour of this sort was extremely laborious to make and thus available to only the richest and most powerful individuals.**

6

EXPANSION AND DECLINE IN EUROPE

There are signs of habitation in Europe before the last Ice Age, but centuries of glaciation made much of the continent uninhabitable and drove the population south towards warmer climates.

Humans are thought to have entered (or perhaps re-entered) Europe around 50,000 years ago, migrating north and west from the Middle East over the next 40,000 years.

The early growth and spread of populations in Europe is difficult to track precisely; distinct cultural groups did not appear at once. There was also a great deal of cultural and genetic mingling even after these distinct groups emerged. The move to an agricultural society allowed populations to expand rapidly and probably contributed to the emergence of distinct groups. As a tribe settled in an area, it would have frequent contact

OPPOSITE: The Picts of Scotland left behind numerous stone carvings that suggest a fairly advanced culture similar to that of the Celts. Lack of written records and later amalgamation into other cultures make it difficult to put these carvings into context, however.

only with the inhabitants of the immediate territory. Over time, these people would develop a culture based on their shared characteristics, and which might be different from that practised by more distant groups.

By around 1000–900 BCE, distinct cultural and genetic groups had appeared in Europe, although as always there was some mingling around the edges. The Celtic or proto-Celtic people came to dominate central and western Europe, with the Iberian Peninsula being home to a mix of Basque and Iberian people.

Scandinavia was dominated by the Germanic tribes, whose language diverged from the Indo-European root around 3000 BCE. This suggests that the Germanic people were a distinct group from that time. They did not, however, dwell in modern Germany. The Germanic homelands were the modern Scandinavian countries (except Finland), from where they migrated into northern Europe at a later date. The Germanic Scandinavians became the ancestors of the Norsemen, or

RIGHT: This rather fanciful depiction of Ancient Britons adorned in woad and armed with anachronistic weaponry is typical of the 'noble savage' concept that predominated for many years. Modern research has shown this image to be highly inaccurate.

Vikings, and shared a number of cultural traits in common with the Celtic people.

To the East of the Celtic homelands, the Slavic and Scythian people dwelled in the region north of the Black Sea, with a mix of Slavs and Finns coming to dominate the Baltic coastal regions. The Finnic people migrated into this area from the Ural mountains, spreading northwards into what is now Finland. Southern and south-eastern Europe also developed their own distinct groups. The Etruscans came to dominate most of Italy, while Greeks, Thracians and Illyrians emerged in south-eastern Europe.

Development of these groups was heavily influenced by their interactions with one another and with other civilizations in the Middle East. Technology, ideas and borrowed words flowed back and forth through trade and conflict. The Greeks were particularly influential in the development of European culture, acting as a filter through which new concepts coming out of the Middle East were fed into European society. Greek traders roamed the Mediterranean and established trade ports, and their influence spread at second hand through the people they traded with into lands where no Greek had set foot.

This may have been a factor in the Celts' lack of a written language of their own. It is often said that they were illiterate, but this is not strictly accurate. The Celts preferred to commit important facts to the memories of their bards and druids than to write them down, but they did use written communication when it suited them. Greek was at that time a common language spoken and read widely across Europe, so when a letter or other communication had to be sent, Greek was the logical choice. Some Celts were literate in Greek (and possibly other languages too) but there was never any real need for a written form of the Celtic spoken language.

ABOVE: **The use of Ogham writing may date from as early as the 1st century CE. Its straight lines are relatively easy to carve into a rock or other hard medium, much like the runes of Scandinavia.**

'IT IS OFTEN SAID THAT THEY WERE ILLITERATE, BUT THIS IS NOT STRICTLY ACCURATE.'

ABOVE: **Celtic warriors formed a large part of the Carthaginian army which invaded the Italian mainland during the Second Punic War. Ultimately Carthage was destroyed and Iberia became a Roman possession despite Celtic resistance.**

The Celtiberians

As already noted, the Celts of central Europe had extensive contact with Greek cities both in south-east Europe and elsewhere around the Mediterranean. A recognizably Celtic society emerged before the beginning of the Iron Age, and by around 1300–1200 BCE it had reached the Iberian Peninsula. Other groups were visiting the British Isles to trade on a fairly frequent basis, and no doubt some of them settled there.

Opinions are divided as to whether there was a major 'Celtic invasion of Spain' or a stream of migrants who brought Celtic culture into the region over an extended period. It is likely that there were waves of migrants, which could constitute an invasion if there was much conflict as a group arrived.

The main Celtic route into Spain was via passes over the eastern Pyrenees. The Celtic 'invaders' then spread themselves out across the Peninsula, mingling with the local population to create the culture that Roman writers would dub Celtiberian. This movement into Iberia brought the Celts into conflict with Carthage, a powerful city-state on the coast of what is today Tunisia.

Carthage was founded around 800 BCE by seagoing traders from Phoenicia, which was situated in modern-day Syria and Lebanon. Although originally intended as little more than a base to resupply and repair ships, the city grew into a major power in its own right, and came to dominate much of the western Mediterranean including what is now southern Spain. Carthaginian expansion into Iberia began around 575 BCE.

Celtic warriors at times served as mercenaries for Carthage, but there was also extensive conflict for control over parts of Iberia. The Celts favoured guerrilla tactics, using lightly equipped forces with good mobility on foot or horseback to strike wherever the Carthaginians were weak. The Celtiberians of this period are recorded as being mainly armed with swords and javelins plus a small round shield, with some using bows or axes in addition.

In 509 BCE, Carthage agreed a treaty of friendship with Rome, which was at the time a small emerging power on the Italian mainland. Roman expansion into the islands of the Mediterranean caused friction that eventually led to open warfare. The First Punic War (between Carthage and Rome) was fought from 264 to 241 BCE, mainly in the region of Sicily and the surrounding seas.

Roman forces did not operate in Iberia during this first of the three Punic Wars against Carthage, and the Celtiberians were not directly involved in the conflict. However, their resistance to Carthaginian expansion in Iberia was a distraction, while the war helped the Celtiberians remain free of Carthaginian influence for a while longer.

After the end of the First Punic War, the Carthaginians were forced to pay a huge tribute to Rome, but this did not prevent new efforts at expanding their territories in Iberia. The Second

BELOW: **The First Punic War between Carthage and Rome took place largely at sea and did not directly affect the Celts of Iberia. Celtic warriors played a much greater part in the Second Punic War, joining Hannibal's invasion of Italy.**

Punic War (218–201 BCE) was triggered by a Carthaginian attack on the independent city of Saguntum. Saguntum asked for help from Rome, which was agreed, but before any aid was sent Carthaginian troops took the city. This damaged Roman prestige, which of course had to be avenged.

Hannibal's Invasion

During the resulting war, Carthaginian forces invaded Roman lands by sea while a major invasion of Italy was mounted by Hannibal Barca. Hannibal's army travelled overland to cross the Alps into northern Italy. This required marching through Celtic lands, and Celtic warriors might have greatly influenced the campaign had they opposed Hannibal in significant numbers. However, many of them did quite the opposite – Hannibal was able to recruit infantry and a small number of horsemen in Iberia, and picked up more as he marched through Gaul.

The Gallic and Celtiberian warriors each had slightly different approaches to battle. The Gauls fought in a typically Celtic manner, preferring to get stuck in as quickly as possible, whereas the Celtiberians took a slightly more thoughtful approach. Their preferred mode of engagement was to hurl javelins en masse and then charge into their reeling opponents. In this their methods were not unlike those of the more disciplined Romans.

The Celtiberians had one other similarity with Roman troops – they favoured a heavy javelin of soft iron called the angon. The angon, like the Roman pilum, was intended to render shields useless by bending when it stuck in them, weighing the shield down and making it impossible to wield.

The Gallic and Celtiberian infantry formed the centre of Hannibal's force at the Battle of Cannae, where they drew the amateurishly led Roman forces into a trap by being slowly pushed back. Celtic horsemen were part of the flanking force that enveloped the Roman wings

BELOW: **Various designs of spear and javelin heads were used, depending on the intended target and local preferences. A broad head caused a wider wound track but would penetrate less easily, making it a less effective weapon against well-protected targets.**

once their centre was deep in the Carthaginian army, contributing to the worst defeat in Roman history. The Celts were also notable for being the only troops on either side wearing trousers.

Despite Hannibal's great victory at Cannae, and his brilliant campaign on Italian soil against superior forces, he was ultimately defeated. In the interim, Roman forces had campaigned in Spain with the intent of removing the Carthaginian presence there. This brought about extensive contact between the local population and the Romans, who applied the label 'Celtiberian' to more or less everyone in the region. In fact the mingled Celtic, Iberian and mixed populations created a confused situation such that it was probably difficult enough for the locals to tell who was a Celt and who was not, so the group label is understandable. It does, however, muddy the waters somewhat regarding the written history of the region.

The first Roman expedition collapsed in 211 BCE when Carthage bribed the large Celtiberian force hired by Rome to desert their allies. This left Roman forces outmatched and resulted in two defeats at related battles collectively known as the Battle of the Upper Baetis.

Rome returned the next year in greater force and was able to defeat the Carthaginian forces in the region without relying heavily on local mercenaries. Carthage, however, was willing to take whatever help was available and continued to hire Celtiberian warriors. In 206 BCE, a Carthaginian force including a large contingent of Celtiberians met a somewhat smaller Roman army at Ilipa. After initial skirmishing and a period of standoff, the Roman force deployed for battle with its best troops facing the undisciplined Celtiberians on the flanks.

ABOVE: **Hannibal's expedition into Italy is primarily famous for the fact that he brought along a force of war elephants. However, his Celtic allies were more militarily significant than the elephants, all of whom died fairly early in the campaign.**

ABOVE: The Celtiberian tribes resisted Roman rule for a time after the fall of Carthage, and retained much of their culture even after conquest. Thereafter, their strength and energy served Rome, providing warlike recruits to the legions raised in the region.

Although the Roman centre, comprised largely of Iberian allies, was weaker than the Carthaginian troops facing it, it was protected by skirmishers who delayed the Carthaginians from making contact. The Roman troops on the flanks were able to defeat their Celtiberian opponents and envelop the Carthaginian flanks. Bad weather allowed the Carthaginians to avoid a reverse of what they had done at Cannae, but that night the Celtiberian contingent sealed the fate of Carthage in Iberia by deserting en masse.

Most of the remaining Carthaginian force was killed or forced to surrender after being cornered by Roman pursuers, after which the Romans took control of Iberia by conquest of the Celtiberians, and exacted vengeance for their part in the war against Rome. Large-scale Celtiberian resistance to Rome went on until around 133 BCE, by which time Carthage had been destroyed in the Third Punic War of 149–146 BCE.

Thereafter the region was a Roman possession, initially divided into two provinces (Hispania Citerior and Hispania Ulterior). It was later subdivided, and remained a Roman province until the fall of the Empire. The last resurgence of Celtiberian independence was in the Sertorian War of 80–72 BCE. This was largely a Roman internal conflict rather than external resistance, but Celtiberian warriors played a major part in the conflict. After the pacification of the region, Hispania remained a Roman possession until the fall of the Empire.

By that time, Celtic, Roman and Iberian cultures had been thoroughly mingled, with an intermixing of others such as that of the Visigoths and Vandals, Germanic people who migrated into the region during the era of great turmoil in Europe precipitated by the Hunnic invasions. Later, Iberia would be invaded by the Moors, coming north from Africa, causing further cultural upheavals.

Celts in Greece and the East

Probably as a result of population expansion, Celtic tribes began to push south and east towards the Balkan region in

significant numbers from around 450 BCE onwards. As with any
migration, the tribes followed predictable, easy routes. While
a small party can cross almost any terrain, a large group or a
whole tribe seeking a new place to live must follow valleys
and passes where there is firewood, food and water to be easily
foraged. Thus the successive Celtic groups that moved into the
Balkan region generally tended to follow the same routes as
their predecessors.

At this time, the northern Balkans and the Danube basin
were inhabited by various tribal groups that were often in
conflict with one another or with the Greeks to the south. This
disorganization allowed the Celts to establish themselves by a mix
of conquest, land seizure or what amounted to armed squatting.
A local tribe that was distracted by conflict elsewhere might find
that a large number of well-armed people had moved into part
of their territory and built settlements. They might be dislodged
by military action but the Celts were warlike and well armed, so
often it would have been more prudent to adjust to the situation
and avoid conflict.

**BELOW: Expansion was
largely dictated by
terrain and the level of
opposition encountered.
Some tribes did fight
their way through
hostile territory to find a
new home, but as a rule
migration took the path
of least resistance.**

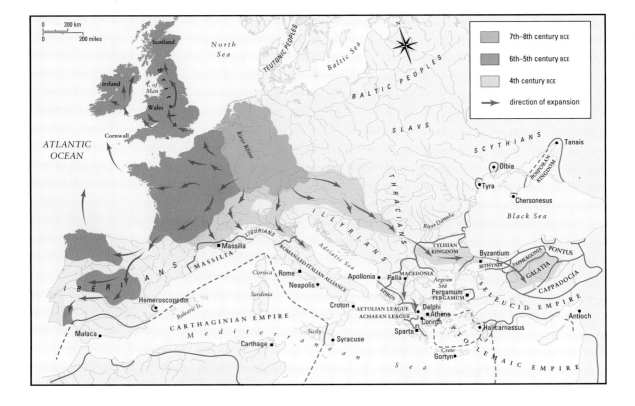

As the Celts insinuated themselves into the local political landscape they grew in power, not least because the fertile local soil could support large populations with ease. Celtic dominance over the region increased over time, but the Danube basin remained an area with a mix of populations, and the Celts were influenced by Greek, Illyrian and Thracian culture even as they placed their own stamp on local affairs.

The Celts of the Danube basin and northern Balkans were familiar with Greek affairs, and indeed sometimes participated in Greek conflicts as mercenaries. They were aware of the wars of Philip of Macedon, which greatly increased the power of his kingdom. The Celts may well have benefited from Philip's wars, as he fought at times against tribes in Illyria and Thrace who might otherwise have opposed Celtic expansion.

Alexander 'The Great'

After the assassination of Philip of Macedon, his son Alexander took the throne in 336 BCE, and the following year the Celts sent a delegation to pay their respects. This led to an agreement between the Celts and Alexander as he set out on the conquests that would lead to him becoming 'The Great'. The Celts helped secure the northern frontiers of Alexander's homeland, largely by warring with others who might invade in his absence, and in return they were spared the need to fight against him.

The deal held until Alexander's death in 323 BCE, after which the Celts began pushing south against the borders of Macedon. A major campaign in 313–310 BCE brought large areas of Illyria under Celtic dominance, subjugating the local tribes, and this in turn caused the Macedonian king, Cassander, to consider the Celts to be a major threat. He inflicted a serious defeat on a Celtic incursion into Macedon in 310 or 298 BCE but could not prevent the Celts from overrunning some areas of Thrace.

Among the enemies faced by the Celts of the Balkan region were some of the successors of Alexander the Great. Known as

ABOVE: **Probably wisely, the Celts of the Balkan region pursued good relations with Alexander the Great. They held his successors in less regard, however, and invaded Macedon soon after Alexander's death.**

the Diadochi, these leaders inherited parts of his empire and strong military forces, but fought against one another as well as external threats and internal dissent in the conquered areas. In Thrace, Lysimachus attempted to build a kingdom while Cassander had Greece and Macedon. Both had to deal with Celtic incursions as well as their own wars.

The death of Cassander in 298 BCE created an opportunity to seize the throne of Macedon. A period of savage infighting among the Diadochi resulted in the death of Lysimachus and the fragmentation of his kingdom, and also the ascendance to the Macedonian throne of Ptolemy Ceranus. The situation in Thrace after the death of Lysimachus allowed the Celts to cause havoc there for several years before they were mostly driven out.

In 279 BCE the Celts of the northern Balkans launched what has been dubbed the Great Expedition. They are often described as being led by someone named Brennos, but there is significant doubt as to whether this individual existed. Be that as it may, the Great Expedition sent contingents against Macedonia, Greece, Thrace and the surrounding lands.

The initial Macedonian response was not successful. The Macedonian army was heavily defeated and their king killed. However, the incursion was turned back soon afterward. There is some debate as to whether the Celts were forcibly driven from Macedonia or simply decided that they had gained sufficient plunder that further fighting was not desirable. Either way, the expedition retired northwards.

A renewed expedition was launched once the various Celtic contingents had regrouped. This was

BELOW: According to legend, the Great Expedition was led by an individual named Brennus or Brennos. There is much doubt as to whether or not he actually existed, however. He may have been a legendary figure composited from real Celtic leaders of the time.

aimed at central Greece, taking a route that travelled through the pass of Thermopylae. The pass was one of the few routes that an army could take in that region, and its natural defensive advantages had made it the site of a famous stand in 480 BCE against Persian invaders.

As before, the pass was held by a coalition of Greek forces, which managed to beat off the initial Celtic attack with heavy casualties. Seeking to weaken the defence, the Celts sent a contingent into nearby Aetolia, which drew off their contingent from the army holding Thermopylae. However, the Aetolians' desperate defence of their homes cost the Celts yet more casualties and the diversionary tactic did not result in a breakthrough.

As in the previous, more famous Battle of Thermopylae, the invaders were eventually able to outflank the defenders and bypass the obstacle. The defenders were evacuated by sea and were able to rejoin the fight later. The Celts marched on Delphi but were repulsed, after which they were heavily defeated at the river Spercheios. This brought the Great Expedition to a close, although some elements of the force did proceed into Thrace where they managed to create a short-lived territory. This was destroyed in 212 BCE.

Some of the Celts driven out of Thrace were not pushed back into the Danube basin but instead settled in Asia Minor, creating the region known as Galatia. The Galatians were culturally Celts with a heavy Greek influence, whose martial prowess allowed them to carve out a substantial territory. Their services as mercenaries or allies were widely sought over the next decades, and Galatian warriors were involved in the many power struggles of the region. They were not averse to joining both sides of a conflict if the payment was good enough, and their influence on regional affairs was great even when they had no agenda of their own.

The Kingdom of Dacia, with its capital here at Sarmisegetusa Regia, was created at the expense of local Celtic tribes. It was the creation of one man, Burebista, and fragmented rapidly after his death in 44 BCE.

However, the Galatians' power eventually declined, notably after serous defeats in battle. In 189 BCE a Roman expeditionary force inflicted two heavy defeats on the Galatians, notably through superior arms and equipment, and they were forced to sue for peace. Galatia then fell under Roman control, and was later annexed by the kingdom of Pontus. The ensuing Mithridatic wars between Rome and Pontus resulted in a Roman victory, and Galatia became a Roman client state.

Hellenized Galatia

Galatia became increasingly Hellenized over time, with its distinctly Celtic cuture gradually melding with the Anatolian way of life. It was recorded around 400 CE that the Galatian language was still extant, but by then the region had lost much of its unique culture and was no longer a 'Celtic' homeland as such.

The Celts of the Danube basin and the surrounding area remained powerful for the next century, although their influence was greatly diminished after defeat at the hands of Dacian and Thracian tribes under the leadership of Burebista. His short-lived ascendency allowed him to conduct raids and conquests from the Danube basin to the Black Sea. The Celtic tribes of the region suffered heavily, and their tribal confederation largely broke up.

OPPOSITE: **The Classical image of the proud (and for whatever reason, naked) Celtic warrior is captured in this statue, which depicts a defeated Galatian warrior killing his wife and then himself rather than be captured alive.**

New tribes seem to appear around this time, possibly as a result of the breakup of the old structure of tribal confederations. A conflicting set of names, imposed perhaps by Roman writers, further confuses the issue. It does seem likely that Germanic tribes were moving into the area during this period, and Roman administrators deliberately relocated tribes into the region to prevent a resurgence of Celtic dominance. This apparently worked; the Celtic tribes of the region were absorbed into a more general population that included Illyrian, Dacian, Thracian and Germanic influences, and as in many other areas it gradually ceased to be purely 'Celtic'.

'MUCH OF WHAT IS KNOWN ABOUT THE CELTS COMES TO US THROUGH GREEK WRITINGS AND IMAGES.'

Much of what is known about the Celts comes to us through Greek writings and images such as statues, based on knowledge gained during this period of Celtic/Greek interaction. Many statues depict naked Celtic warriors, but it is not clear whether this is an accurate representation of someone who – for whatever reason – chose to go about his business naked, or whether it is due to Greek fashion. Naked statues are very common in Greek-influenced areas, so perhaps the idea of the Celtic warrior running naked into battle is no more than a distortion caused by stylized representation.

Whether or not it is true that Greek writings and statues have distorted our impression of the Celts, it is certain that the Celts influenced events in the Greek world. Their wars with the enemies of Macedon, and their participation in the conflicts among Alexander's successors, exerted an influence on the course of history that cannot easily be fathomed. It might be that without Celts in the Balkans, Alexander's enormous empire might not have been carved out, and without their involvement in its aftermath the legacy of that empire could have been quite different.

Celts in Cisalpine Gaul and Central Europe

The original homeland of the Celts is sometimes assumed to be central Europe, not least because this is where the Hallstatt and La Tène archaeological sites were found. However, there is evidence that the proto-Celts migrated into this area from a region much further east. Be that as it may, recognizably Celtic culture had a major centre in what is now Austria and the surrounding region. The proto-Celts had been settled in this area for some time when their true Celtic culture emerged.

From this central point, groups spread out in all directions, some of them finding their way into the British Isles, Iberia and other distant places. Movement across the north European plain was relatively easy, allowing large groups to migrate to find new homes, traders to move their wares easily and military forces to both march and forage effectively. As a result the Celts spread northwards to the North Sea coast, settling in modern-day Belgium and the Netherlands, and westwards into what is now France.

To the north, the Celts encountered the Germanic people of the Baltic region, notably in Denmark. Most of the historical data we have on this era is of Roman origin, and is in many cases based on hearsay or incomplete information – or misunderstandings of that information. Roman sources are often not especially clear

BELOW: A stereotypical image of civilized Romans battling the savage Celts. The 'barbarians' are ill-armed and half-dressed wild men (and women), contrasted with the well organized and equipped forces of civilization.

on the differences between the Gallic (i.e. Celtic) tribes and the Germanic tribes. The Roman viewpoint seems to have been that anyone living east of the Rhine was Germanic; a homeland west of it made one a Gaul. The Romans also apparently considered Germanic warriors to be fiercer than Gauls.

This rather vague distinction served Roman interests well enough – they cared about the political situation as it affected Rome, not the cultural and genetic heritage of the people along their borders. In Roman usage, the term Germania referred to a specific region west of the Rhine and Germani to a group of tribes that lived in the area. Modern references to the Germanic people of Scandinavia reflect a different use of the name.

BELOW: The Senone chieftain (foreground) wears distinctly Romanized war gear while his Gaulish counterpart is dressed in more traditionally Celtic fashion. Both retain a preference for the long cutting sword as a personal weapon.

Contact with the Germanic people of Denmark resulted in trade, exchange of ideas and some words, and the usual mix of violence and intermarriage. The Celts and the Scandinavians interacted to at least some degree; some cultural practices are quite similar and there seems to have been a fair amount of trade in goods. Similarly, the Celts interacted and intermixed with the Finns and Slavs to their east. This would create a gradual fading of 'Celticness' the farther north or east one went.

In what is now France, the Celts were able to spread out and settle wherever they would. On the Mediterranean coast they came into contact with Greek traders, which opened up new possibilities for the tribes nearby. Goods from the coast found their way inland, and warriors from the inland tribes journeyed to the coast to take service as mercenaries. Meanwhile the Celtic tribes settled into their new homes in France and quickly came to dominate the region.

The Senones

Movement southwards across the Alps was more of a problem, and it was not until around 400 BCE that significant numbers of Celts made the migration. The first tribe to come into contact with Rome was the Senones, who crossed into northern Italy and began seeking a home. This brought them into conflict with the Etruscans of northern Italy, and they in turn requested Roman assistance.

The ensuing war resulted in Rome being sacked by the Senones, but they could not hold it and instead retired northwards to settle in less well defended lands. The Senones remained a threat to Rome for many years; conflict went on sporadically until 283 BCE, when the Senones were finally defeated and driven from Italy. By this time the Roman military system had evolved from a basically Greek-style phalanx to the more flexible legion model.

The Romans referred to the Celts they encountered as Gauls, and their homelands were known by the same name. The Celtic lands south of the Alps were known as Gallia Cisalpina (or Cisalpine Gaul), while the lands of the Gauls beyond the Aps were known as Gallia Transalpina (Transalpine Gaul). Roman expansion was at first confined to Italy, which was home to numerous Greek and Italian city-states as well as tribal groups such as the Samnites. Conflict with these absorbed much of Roman attention for many decades, allowing the Gauls of northern Italy to establish themselves.

Shortly after expelling the Senones and annexing Cisalpine Gaul, Rome came into conflict with the Italian city-state of Tarentum, and then with the northwestern Greek state of Epirus. This conflict went on until 275 BCE and probably delayed Roman expansion northwards for some time.

ABOVE: Although the Gauls generally preferred to fight on foot, many warriors owned horses and would fight from horseback when they had to. Forces of Gaulish cavalry proved effective in battles against Rome, though for the most part the conquest of Gaul was an infantry-versus-infantry affair.

The Senones' incursion into Cisalpine Gaul was followed by a migration of the Boii tribal group, who entered Italy from the northeast and took over some formerly Etruscan territory. The Boii fought alongside the Senones against Rome, inflicting a defeat on Roman forces at Arretium in 284 BCE. Allying with the Etruscans, they launched a major campaign against Rome in 283 BCE, where they were also assisted by mercenaries from the Senones tribe.

Sending warriors to fight against Rome, even as mercenaries, was a violation of the Senones' treaty with Rome. However, such was the ill-feeling between the two that when Roman emissaries came to the tribe to demand the mercenaries' recall, the Senones murdered them. They concealed the deed by scattering the emissaries' bodies in small pieces. Unsurprisingly, perhaps, the Romans were not deceived and launched an expedition against the Senones, whose fighting power was reduced by the absence of some of their warriors.

The Senones were heavily defeated, with many survivors executed or sold into slavery, and the survivors scattered. The mercenaries still serving with the Boii attempted to take vengeance in battle but were also defeated; many killed themselves rather than submit to Rome.

BELOW: Many Gauls preferred to kill themselves rather than surrender to Rome. In many cases a quick suicide was preferable to the cruel execution methods favoured by the Romans, especially for warriors who believed that their lives would go on elsewhere after death.

Boii Campaign

The Boii remained a power in northeastern Italy, growing in influence until they threatened all the existing powers in Italy. In 225 BCE they hired mercenaries from Transalpine Gaul for a new campaign in Italy. In response, a Roman-led coalition, which included Etruscan and Samnite forces, among others, sent an army against the Gauls.

Attempting to avoid battle, the Gallic army crossed the Apennines into Etruria and plundered the region. Roman forces made contact near Clusium, whereupon the Gauls began to retire. An over-hasty pursuit drew the Romans into an ambush, resulting in a heavy defeat. However, Roman reinforcements arrived and a second battle was fought, this time near Telamon.

The Gauls were defeated, not least due to Roman superiority in close combat. The heavy armour and close-range killing power of the Roman sword proved more effective than the Gauls' slashing

'THEY CONCEALED THE DEED BY SCATTERING THE EMISSARIES' BODIES IN SMALL PIECES.'

weapons and light or no body protection, and despite a hard fight the majority of the Gallic force was slain or taken prisoner.

This campaign was significant for several reasons. It proved the superiority of current Roman military methods over those of their 'barbarian' opponents, and not coincidentally perhaps it was the last occasion when Celts attempted to use chariots in warfare on mainland Europe. The battle also permitted a punitive expedition to be launched against the weakened Boii. This greatly diminished their power, although it was not the end of their time in northern Italy.

There were wider implications of this campaign, beyond removing the threat of the Boii and their mercenaries. In order to have stability elsewhere, Rome made a treaty with Carthage effectively giving up any territorial claims or interests in Iberia. This freed up Roman forces that might otherwise have had to guard against Carthaginian movements, but did increase the power of Carthage at a time when conflict was becoming inevitable.

The Boii were eventually driven from Italy after further defeats in 194 and 193 BCE, mostly moving north-east around the Adriatic Sea to settle in the Danube basin. There, they regained some of their power until their tribal confederation was broken up in a series of conflicts starting around 60 BCE. A splinter group of the Boii accompanied the migration of the Helvetii and were involved in the Gallic wars that resulted.

The Gaesatae

Among the other Gallic populations in Italy were the Gaesatae, who often fought as mercenaries alongside other tribes.

Indeed, some ancient historians translated their tribal name as 'mercenaries' although 'spearmen' or 'javelinmen' is probably a better translation. The Gaesatae are recorded as fighting naked, and some sources note that this was in contrast to their clothed allies. Polybius claims that this was to prevent their clothing from being damaged if it snagged on brambles, an assertion that raises some questions. It is debatable whether anyone, clothed or not, would try to fight amid brambles, and if this did occurr then one must wonder how effective a naked man can be while trying to wield a sword among sharp thorns.

Such is the nature of ancient writings. Less open to question is the assertion that the Gaesatae favoured small shields and little or no other protection, and were easy prey for Roman javelins. For all their skill and fervour the Gaesatae were unable to make much difference to the military balance in Italy. Among those that hired them were the Insubre, who appear to be a 'Celticized' local tribe rather than migrating Celts.

BELOW: **It is not surprising that carvings depicting Romans battling Gauls are extremely common. The Gauls were a constant threat for much of the history of Rome, and were involved on almost all occasions when Rome itself was seriously threatened.**

The lands of the Insubre lay in northwest Italy and were subject to frequent Celtic incursions as well as ongoing small-scale migration and trade. As a result their culture acquired a Celtic flavour with influences from other Italian groups such as the Etruscans. The Insubres opposed Roman expansion and, along with the Boii, were part of the army that was defeated by Roman forces at Telamon in 225 BCE.

By 221 BCE, the Insubres had been subjugated by Rome and were forced into an alliance that lasted until 218 BCE when

Hannibal's Carthaginian army entered their territory. The Insubres rebelled against Rome and assisted the Carthaginians until 194 BCE when they entered into a new and lasting alliance with Rome. Their culture became increasingly Romanized and by 49 BCE the region was granted full Roman citizenship.

The only Gallic tribe in Italy that seems to have been consistently pro-Roman was the Cenomani. They followed the Senones into Italy and settled on land seized from the Etruscans, but became friendly with Rome where other Celtic tribes more or less continuously fought against her. The Cenomani and their allies, the Veneti, were on the winning side when the Boii and their allies were defeated in 225 BCE, and also initially sided with Rome when Carthaginian forces invaded Italy starting in 218 BCE. A brief rebellion in 200 BCE was soon quelled, and the Cenomani returned to their old allegiance. As with other former Celts in Cisalpine Gaul, the Cenomani were awarded full Roman citizenship in 49 BCE.

Although not pro-Roman as such, elements of the Volcae chose to join the Roman Republic rather than being conquered. Two branches of the Volcae existed in the region between the Garonne and Rhone rivers, with another in the Danube region.

The latter were involved in Celtic incursions into Greece and were very powerful until sometime in the first century BCE when they were eclipsed by Germanic and Dacian rivals. The Volcae of Gaul had two branches. The Volcae Arecomici had capitals at what are now Nimes and Narbonne, and presumably had considerable contact with Rome. As the Roman Republic expanded its influence into their region, the Arecomici chose to join it. It is possible that this decision was influenced by the concept that it was better to join than to be forcibly incorporated. The economic and political benefits of friendship with Rome were considerable, those that resisted expansion had a tendency to become 'friends' anyway, although of a lower-status sort.

ABOVE: **A gold coin minted by the Aulerci Cenomani tribe of Gaul. The value of coins depended on the quality and weight of metal contained in them rather than some arbitrary standard. The value of any given tribe's coinage could thus vary considerably.**

Thus, in 121 BCE the Volcae Arecomici went from being an independent Celtic tribe to being the citizens of the Roman province of Gallia Narbonensis, who just happened to be of Celtic origin and whose culture was still definitively Celtic. It is interesting to note that the city of Narbonne is cited as being founded by Roman colonists in 118 BCE, three years after the Volcae Arecomici joined the Republic. Their settlement at Narbonne may have been incorporated into the Roman colony or they may have joined the new colony as it expanded.

The related Volcae Tectosages remained outside the Roman Republic for almost another century. This was partly by reason of geography. The Volcae Tectosages had their capital at Tolosa, which is now Toulouse, beyond the sphere of Roman influence at that time. They had dealings with the Carthaginians in Iberia and at times sent mercenaries to fight for Carthage. Their independence ended in 105 BCE as a result of antagonizing Rome.

Volcae warriors joined other Gauls in fighting alongside Germanic invaders, triggering a Roman response that was soundly defeated at Tolosa in 107 BCE. A punitive expedition sacked the city, after which the Volcae Tectosages became Roman subjects. Among the loot plundered from Tolosa was a large quantity of gold said to have been looted from Delphi during the Celtic expeditions into Greece in 217 BCE. The gold was supposedly cursed, and mysteriously disappeared after the force transporting it was attacked en route – although interestingly silver looted from Tolosa arrived safely in Rome.

The Volcae Tectosages, like many other tribes of the region, became part of the Roman expansion. However, other branches of the tribe survived elsewhere, notably in Germania and Galatia. This movement and splintering of tribes makes it difficult to track their history as they can appear to be in several places at once, but it also means that a tribe might survive in some form even if its main branch were destroyed or conquered.

Melded into Europe

From their emergence as an Iron Age people around 800 BCE, the Celts enjoyed several centuries of ascendance in Europe and even beyond. Their trading acumen and swordsmanship influenced affairs from Iberia to Asia Minor, and helped shape the course of the death-struggle between Rome and Carthage. The Celtic groups outside Gaul and the British Isles were gradually weakened and absorbed or altered into something that was no longer truly Celtic, but they were not crushed or destroyed. Instead the Celts melded into the emerging future of Europe and influenced it from within rather than standing as a power in their own right. It is impossible to see where that influence ended, if indeed it ever did.

BELOW: Excavations at the Clos de la Lombarde in Narbonne have not confirmed whether the city was founded by Romans or Gauls; the two cultures melded over the centuries until it is not possible to see where one ends and the other begins.

7

THE CELTS IN GAUL

Gaul (i.e. modern-day France and the North Sea coast) became home to a great many Celtic tribes, of which significant numbers were grouped into tribal confederations.

These were loosely organized for the most part, built around bonds of kinship, traditional friendship or simply geographic proximity. Elements of these confederations at times broke off or wandered into new areas as a result of a defeat in battle. Other groups migrated over significant distances, further complicating the task of cataloguing the many tribes and confederations. The tribes followed a generally similar lifestyle and organization, sufficiently so that outsiders such as the Romans could not always tell the difference between tribes.

This problem has continued ever since. For example the Belgae of what is today Belgium are described as being Gauls who are not quite the same as the 'Celtic' Gauls. Their origins may have been Germanic, although here too there are questions to be asked about what exactly made a tribe Germanic and

OPPOSITE: The best-known of all Gaulish leaders was Vercingetorix, who led the resistance to Julius Caesar's Gallic campaign. Although a very charismatic and well-respected leader, he was not the commander of a unified force. Ultimately, superior Roman organization prevailed over Gaulish courage.

another Celtic. What is known is that the Belgae were fearsome warriors who were known for their impressive rages, and that by the time of Caesar's Gallic Wars their speech and way of life were a close match to those of their Celtic neighbours.

The Belgae

The Belgae were a tribal confederation whose members did not necessarily have the same origins. It is thought that many of the Belgae may have migrated across the Rhine from 'Germanic' lands at least as early as the third century BCE. They probably intermarried with the local Celtic tribes, and cultural exchanges would result in a Celtic way of life. However, Caesar records that the Belgae were the most warlike and ferocious of the Gauls. Similarly he claims that Germanic warriors were fiercer than their Gallic equivalents, which correlates to the idea of the Belgae as Celticized Germanics.

ABOVE: **Statues such as these, from around 200 BCE, give an indication of what the Gauls looked and dressed like. However, fine details and colours must be inferred from other sources such as fragments of cloth that have somehow been preserved.**

There is much debate about the issue of Belgae as true Celts or something slightly different, and even if the question is ever answered it will not have a simple solution. Cultural and genetic intermingling make it difficult to draw neat lines defining who is a Celt and who is not, and the rather simplistic Roman approach of considering anyone east of the Rhine a Gaul is not always helpful. The Belgae and other Gauls, of course, would not have cared much about such things. They defined themselves by family, tribe and tribal confederation rather than some nebulous concept of cultural-genetic groupings. Just as significantly, they did not create clear records of their history.

The Celts of Gaul went about their own affairs for many years, and did not leave much in the way of records for future generations. It is possible to assume, and there is archaeological evidence in many cases, that tribal confederations warred with one another, concluded pacts and merged with others. There was also conflict with outsiders, although the details of this must in many cases be inferred.

Celtic Dominance of Gaul

In the early years of Celtic ascendancy in Gaul, the Bituriges tribe was extremely powerful, but around 500 BCE the tribe split in two. One fragment had its capital at Avaricum (modern Bourges) and the other at Bordeaux. Even as late as the last century BCE, the Bituriges are recorded as being extremely powerful in terms of political, military and druidic influence. Yet such were the changing fortunes of the Gallic tribes that by 60 BCE or so they had fallen heavily under the influence of the Aedui.

Relatively little is known about the affairs of some Gallic tribes, even though in many cases they were large and influential. The Parisii tribe does not appear in many records, other than the facts that they were related to the Senones and may have taken some of them in when the Senones were driven from Italy.

The main claim to fame among the Parisii was the name of their capital, which is modern Paris. The Parisii apparently offered little or no resistance to Roman conquest of Gaul, other than a brief flicker when they sent warriors to the attempted relief of Alesia. This seems to have been forgiven by the Romans, as the Parisii retained their territory and do not seem to have been punished. Indeed, the Parisii capital became an important economic and political centre after Gaul was conquered by Rome, and would ultimately become the capital of a nation.

Other tribes had mixed fortunes over the years. One such was the Averni. In the third and second centuries BCE they were extremely powerful; perhaps the most influential tribe in all of Gaul. This came to an end in 123 BCE when they were defeated along with their

BELOW: Stone carvings can be as difficult to interpret as statutes. Often there are differences of opinion as to what any given object in a carving might be, and conclusions drawn from such sources sometimes remain 'known facts' well after the interpretation is shown to be incorrect.

allies the Allobriges by Roman forces. This came about largely due to Roman fears that the local tribes were a threat to their expansion into the region they now called Gallia Narbonensis. This was essentially the coastal strip from the Alps to the Pyrenees formerly known as Gallia Transalpina.

Roman settlement of the area eclipsed the trading port of Massilia to some extent; the new provincial capital of Narbonne became the main conduit for trade between the Gauls and Rome. It was also the jumping-off point for Caesar's Gallic campaign, and before that the scene of a major incident that marked a change in Roman affairs – with significant consequences for the Gauls. This was the clash between a newly reformed Roman army and an invading Germanic host.

Germanic Influences

Shortly before 112 BCE, the Cimbri, the Ambrones and the Teutones, Germanic tribes from Jutland, migrated south into Celtic lands. Entering the Danube basin they encountered

BELOW: The main Celtic tribes and tribal confederations are relatively easy to define by region. However, there are splinters of these groups, often with the same name, also in quite distant regions. This is sometimes due to displacement or migration, sometimes to identification errors on the part of outside observers.

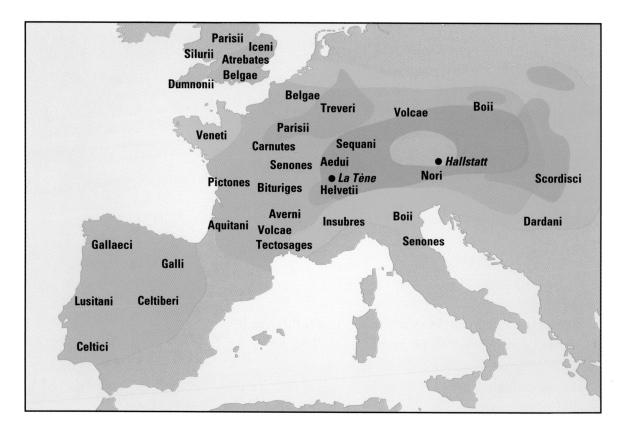

LEFT: The Germanic tribes looked, acted and fought a lot like Celts, but were considered to be more fearsome by their Roman opponents. This is perhaps borne out by the fact that Germania successfully resisted Roman incursions, though terrain also played a part.

resistance from the Celtic tribes of the area including the Nori and Scordisci. Unable to effectively oppose the huge Germanic host, the Celts of the region requested Roman assistance. A Roman army was sent to help, and negotiations from a position of strength resulted in an agreement to withdraw. The Romans, however, then decided to ambush and destroy the Germanic force and were all but annihilated in the resulting battle.

The Germanic tribes then marched west into Gaul where they marauded and pillaged for some years. There are few records of their progress, but there is evidence that they covered a lot of ground – and much of it would have been contested. Eventually part of the Germanic host moved into northern Iberia before finally looping back towards Roman territory.

Not all of the Germanic interactions with the Celts of Gaul were violent or negative; they formed alliances with some tribes, and others took the opportunity afforded by Roman defeats to distance themselves from Roman influence. At least one tribe, the Tigurni, actively allied with the invaders and fought alongside them against Roman forces.

The Germanic incursion was finally defeated in a series of battles, although not all of them went well for Rome. In 107 BCE a Roman army sent to assist one of their allied Gallic tribes was soundly defeated by the Tigurni, which triggered a widespread revolt. This was largely put down by Roman forces,

ABOVE: **Roman accounts of the Battle of Vercellae are enormously exaggerated, but there is evidence that it was a major engagement in which the Germanic force was utterly defeated. The Cimbri tribe virtually ceased to exist, with those not slain sold into slavery.**

but the Germanic threat remained at large. In 105 BCE a Roman army beset by internal politics was routed at Arausio, creating fears that an invasion of Italy was imminent.

The Roman response to this very significant threat was to reorganize their military system, creating the professional army that would later carve out and defend their empire – and which would systematically destroy the Celtic tribes in Gaul and parts of the British Isles. However, at this time the Romans were more concerned with staving off defeat.

The new Roman army took a highly cautious approach to its campaign against the Germanic invaders and their allies, finally inflicting defeats at Aquae Sextiae in 102 BCE and Vercellae in 101 BCE. This conflict, although not directly between Celts and Rome, had important consequences for Gaul. Many Gallic tribes, which had been friendly to Rome, reconsidered their position and entered into conflicts that did not end with the defeat of the Germanic invasion. Memories of victories and defeats – and treatment received in the wake of both – coloured Gallic/Roman interactions thereafter.

Roman attitudes to the Gauls were also affected, perhaps creating a culture of Gallophobia among segments of Roman citizenry that made the campaigns of Julius Caesar more acceptable to the average Roman. At the same time, the invasion and the additional minor conflicts it caused created the instrument of Empire that Julius Caesar's Imperial successors would use to conquer Gaul and the lands beyond.

The Germanic invasion (sometimes called the Cimbrian War in Roman histories) was not the first conflict between Rome and the Gauls who lived beyond the Alps. However, Roman expansion in that direction had not been particularly rapid, and in many cases the Celtic tribes along the borders had cordial relations with the Roman Republic. The Aedui, who occupied much of what is now Burgundy, were Roman allies and became quite heavily Romanized, although this did not prevent them from joining the general Gallic cause during Caesar's Gallic Wars.

The Gallic Wars Begin

Before his campaigns in Gaul, which lasted from 58 to 50 BCE, Julius Caesar was simply one of many influential and powerful political figures in Rome. His own account of his 'Gallic Wars' is somewhat self-glorifying, as might be expected, but it does paint a picture of the Celts in Gaul around this time.

Caesar's decision to invade Gaul was 'sold' to the Roman people as a necessary pre-emptive strike against the dangerous barbarians to the north, and there was some truth in this. However, the conquest of the Gauls and the destruction of the Celtic way of life on the continent was motivated mainly by the ambitions of one man. Put simply, Julius Caesar needed an enemy to defeat in order to win popular acclaim and plunder with which to pay off his enormous debts.

In this he was spectacularly successful. Caesar's campaign in Gaul was characterized by an extreme case of 'mission creep'. Far from being satisfied with his early goals, his success led to a desire for more, and then to a need to deal with the fallout from his aggression. By the time he was finished, Gaul was a Roman possession and Caesar was a popular hero in Rome. So popular did he become that his enemies issued an order for him to return to Rome, prompting the fateful decision to cross the Rubicon into Italy with his legions. The resulting events altered the nature of Roman society, but by that time Gaul had been forever changed.

Caesar's opportunity to pick a fight with the Gauls came when the Helvetii tribal confederation began to migrate from what is now Switzerland towards Gaul. They requested Roman permission to do so, and made promises not to molest

BELOW: Julius Caesar's campaigns in Gaul crushed the Celtic tribes and brought them under Roman rule, and at the same time set the stage for the move from republic to empire. Experience gained against the Gauls was invaluable to Caesar's army in the Roman civil war that followed.

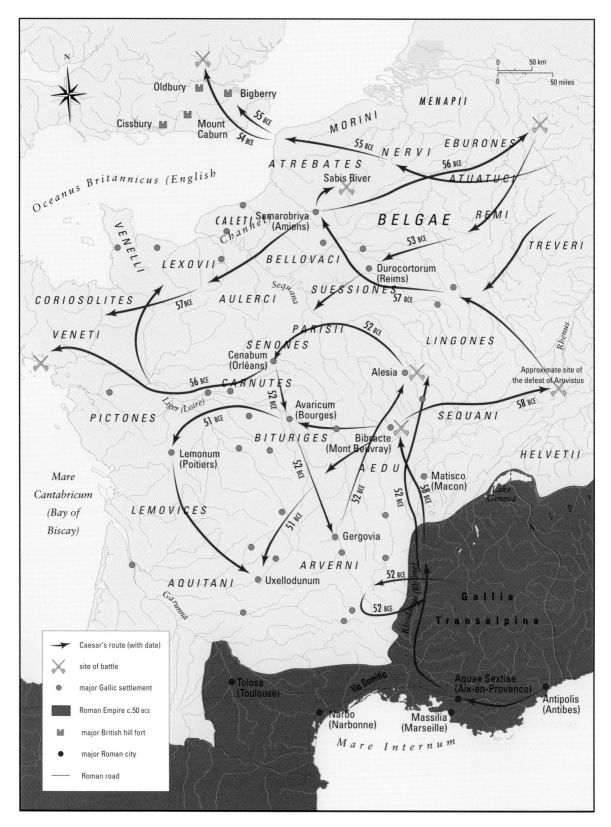

Oldbury · Bigberry

Cissbury · Mount Caburn

MENAPII

MORINI

NERVI   *EBURONES*

ATUATUCI

55 BCE

54 BCE   55 BCE

56 BCE

ATREBATES

Sabis River

REMI

Oceanus Britannicus (English

CALETI

Channel)   Samarobriva
(Amiens)

BELGAE

TREVERI

53 BCE

VENELLI

LEXOVII   *BELLOVACI*

Durocortorum
(Reims)

CORIOSOLITES

AULERCI   *Sequana*   *SUESSIONES*

57 BCE   57 BCE

Rhenus

VENETI

57 BCE

PARISII

52 BCE

LINGONES

SENONES

Cenabum
(Orléans)

Alesia

Approximate site of
the defeat of Arovistus

56 BCE   *CARNUTES*

52 BCE

Avaricum
(Bourges)

Bibracte
(Mont Beuvray)

SEQUANI   58 BCE

Liger (Loire)

PICTONES

51 BCE   *BITURIGES*

AEDU

HELVETII

Lemonum
(Poitiers)

52 BCE

Matisco
(Macon)   58 BCE   Lake
Geneva

Mare

Cantabricum

(Bay of

Biscay)

LEMOVICES

51 BCE

52 BCE   52 BCE   52 BCE

A L P S

51 BCE

Gergovia

52 BCE   *Rhône)*

Gallia

AQUITANI

ARVERNI

Uxellodunum

52 BCE

52 BCE   *Rhodanus (Rhône)*

Transalpina

Garunna

52 BCE

Via Domitia

Aquae Sextiae
(Aix-en-Provence)

Tolosa
(Toulouse)

Antipolis
(Antibes)

Narbo
(Narbonne)

Massilia
(Marseille)

Mare   Internum

Legend:
→ Caesar's route (with date)
✗ site of battle
● major Gallic settlement
▓ Roman Empire c.50 BCE
🏰 major British hill fort
● major Roman city
— Roman road

0 ___ 50 km
0 ___ 50 miles

Roman-allied tribes along the way. Julius Caesar was at the time governor of both Transalpine and Cisalpine Gaul, and thus had a legitimate interest in whether or not a large number of 'barbarians' should be allowed to march through his provinces.

Caesar took this for all it was worth. He negotiated with the Helvetii, although only for the purposes of stalling them while he prepared for a campaign against them. He mustered large forces and fortified river crossings, forcing the Helvetii to take a different route. This brought them into the lands of the Aedui and Allobriges, who were

> **'THEY REQUESTED ROMAN ASSISTANCE, FURTHER LEGITIMIZING CAESAR'S INTERVENTION.'**

friendly with Rome. They requested Roman assistance, further legitimizing Caesar's intervention, and he marched to catch up with the Helvetii at the head of five legions.

The Allobriges, whose territory lay between the Rhone valley and part of what is now Switzerland, were one of the tribes threatened by the Helvetii. They controlled several of the main Alpine passes, which was a source of revenue as well as political power. The Allobriges fought against Hannibal's Carthaginian incursion across the Alps but later came into conflict with Rome. This occurred around 123 BCE and reflects the relative status of a powerful Gallic tribe and the Roman Republic of the time.

The Allobriges gave shelter to members of another tribe that had been defeated by Roman forces, and felt powerful enough to refuse Roman demands to surrender the refugees. They were defeated in 121 BCE and subjected to heavy tribute as punishment, yet remained powerful enough to be involved in Roman politics. The tribe sided with Rome when Julius Caesar launched his Gallic campaign, and their requests for Roman assistance helped legitimize Caesar's questionable actions.

Caesar and his legions caught the Helvetii as they were crossing the River Arar, which was no minor undertaking for such a large migration. Here, the first battle of the Gallic Wars was fought, with a large segment of the Helvetii annihilated. The remainder were able to move on before Caesar's force bridged the river and pursued them. However, Caesar's army ran short

OPPOSITE: **Caesar's Gallic campaigns covered much of what is now France, with excursions across the Rhine and even the English Channel. Much of this activity was political showboating, intended to increase Caesar's status in Rome, though reacting to the uprisings he triggered also motivated many of his movements.**

of supplies and began to march towards Bibracte, capital of the Aedui. This prompted the Helvetii to launch an attack on the Roman force.

The Helvetii came close to defeating the Roman army, but ultimately were unable to break Caesar's defensive position and were worn down. The Helvetii were forcibly relocated back to the homeland they had left, which then had to be resettled as they had burned their homes before marching off. Forcing the Helvetii to remain in their Alpine homeland placed them between Roman territory and the aggressive Germanic tribes to the north. Attacks by the latter were one reason for the Helvetii migration, and no Roman politician wanted Germanic tribes moving into the lands thus vacated.

Germanic and Belgic Involvement

In the wake of Caesar's victory over the Helvetii, several Gallic tribes asked for assistance against Germanic incursions. This created a complex political question, as the Aedui (who were asking for help) were long-standing allies of Rome, but their enemy, the Suebi, had recently been named a 'friend of Rome'. Caesar resolved this by demanding that the Germanic tribes stay on 'their' side of the Rhine. When this was ignored, he had a pretext to wage war against them.

After a period of negotiations, the Roman and Germanic forces fought a hard battle that resulted in massive losses on the Germanic side and the retreat of the surviving Suebi across the Rhine. Although not directly involving the Gauls this action had implications for their future as it encouraged Caesar to continue his

BELOW: The decision of the Helvetii to migrate was not taken lightly, but after much debate it was agreed that the tribes would abandon their lands and destroy their homes to prevent anyone seeking to return to them.

F. RAVEL

campaigns and increased his stature in Roman politics. It also set a precedent for Roman involvement in the affairs of Gauls and other tribal groups.

In 57 BCE, Caesar took advantage of the usual inter-tribal conflicts to march against the Belgae. Among his enemies were the Menapii and the much larger Morini tribes as well as the pre-eminent Nervii. The latter were considered to be the best fighters among all the Gauls by Caesar. They are also recorded as being in some ways rather primitive, in that they had no merchants and did not trade. Nor did they consume alcohol, seeing it as a luxury that would weaken their warlike spirits.

The Nervii led an ambush of Caesar's army near the river Sabis, attacking from the forest with such speed and aggression that the Romans were caught unprepared. This violent assault came close to breaking the Roman army, and Caesar himself is recorded as fighting in the ranks to stave off disaster. The arrival of additional Roman legions, which had been protecting the army's baggage train, stabilized the situation but even so victory was by no means assured. The Nervii seem not to have been

ABOVE: **Ariovistus brought his forces across the Rhine in response to a request for aid in an internal Gaulish conflict. The fact his opponents, the Aedui, were Roman allies in turn triggered Roman involvement, escalating the matter far beyond a simple inter-tribal clash.**

inclined to break off the action, and the Romans were not given the opportunity to do so. The result was close-fought battle that inflicted massive casualties on the Nervii.

Although these losses pacified the Nervii for a while, they recovered in time to join the Gallic revolt of 53 BCE. Along with other Belgic tribes they sent warriors to fight alongside Vercingetorix and his army. Nervii warriors besieged a legion they caught in its winter camp, forcing Caesar to come to the rescue.

Also involved in the Belgic alliance were the Treveri, who were considered to be the best cavalry in Gaul. The Treveri were staunch opponents of Rome during the 57 BCE campaign, fighting on after the defeat of the Nervii and their allies at the battle of the river Sabis. A peace agreement allowed the Treveri to withdraw from the fighting in Gaul, and by 54 BCE a pro-Roman faction had emerged in tribal politics. This was broken, and the Treveri took the field again against Rome, with some success. It is possible that some of the Treveri migrated into Germania around this time. The remaining Treveri were pacified for a time, but revolted in 30 BCE. This was one of the events that caused Rome to tighten its grasp on Gaul and prompted a reorganization of the Gaulish provinces.

'THE CONQUEST OR ANNEXATION OF THE VENETI WAS INEVITABLE SOONER OR LATER.'

The Annexation of Armorica

Although rarely considered a seafaring people, a group as widespread as the Celts were inevitably subject to a great deal of variation and did include some tribes noted for their maritime prowess. Among these were the Veneti of Armorica. Dwelling along the coasts of north-western France, the Veneti were well positioned to trade with Iberia and the British Isles and to demand tolls from any other mariners who wanted to travel along the coast. In an age where oceanic navigation was not possible, this meant that the Veneti largely controlled sea trade between the Mediterranean and the British Isles.

The Veneti had considerable dealings with their Celtic cousins in Britain, and were on sufficiently good terms with many of the tribes there that they were able to request aid against Rome. This began in 57 BCE when, as part of his conquest of Gaul, Julius Caesar demanded the submission of the Veneti. They complied, but a year later they joined the Gallic coalition against Rome.

The conquest or annexation of the Veneti was inevitable sooner or later, given that they controlled the coastal trade routes and posed a threat to Roman shipping in the area, so joining the fight while it looked winnable made sense. The Veneti position was strong; their lands were accessible only by sea or by moving through a largely hostile Gaul, and their settlements were well protected.

At sea, the Veneti were superior in terms of ship design and seamanship. Their robust vessels could resist a ramming attack even if they could not outmanoeuvre their opponents, and the Veneti were skilled at using projectiles from their high-sided vessels. Their knowledge of local waters also provided a strategic advantage. However, the Roman fleet was eventually victorious, opening the way for an amphibious invasion of the Veneti lands. Those of the Veneti that were not massacred were sold into slavery, which not only destroyed the tribe but also removed a major obstacle to the Roman invasion of Britain.

BELOW: The ships of the Veneti were superior to those of Rome, and they were more skilled mariners as well. However, a change in Roman tactics eventually led to victory at the Battle of Morbihan and the breaking of Veneti sea power.

After the defeat of the Veneti, the other tribes of Armorica remained opposed to Rome, although morale was shaken by the defeat and massacre of a powerful tribe. A Roman force pushed into Armorica to pacify the local tribes, who had united under the chieftain of the Unelli tribe. Roman progress took the form of a moving standoff, with the Celts following and harassing the Roman force but unable to mount a large enough attack to defeat it. Instead they hoped to wear the Romans down with constant nuisance attacks and the strain of operating deep in enemy territory.

This strain was made worse by the Celts' habit of taunting their enemies, riding up to their fortified camps and brazenly hurling insults as well as the odd projectile at the surrounded Romans. The strategy actually worked to some extent, but fell foul of a Roman ruse. Feigning panic among the ranks, the Romans showed their tormentors what they hoped and expected to see – a collapsing Roman force ripe for destruction. This drew a disorganized general assault from the Celts, which was met with a carefully timed counter-blow. Celtic morale collapsed at seeing certain victory replaced with a desperate fight, and large segments of the Celtic force were killed or captured. The Armorican tribes surrendered soon afterward, although in 52 BCE they joined the revolt against Rome led by Vercingetorix.

To the south of the Veneti, along the Bay of

BELOW: **The first Roman incursion into Britain was met at the beaches by a Celtic force equipped with large numbers of chariots. Caesar's army eventually established a beachhead, but no real progress was made inland despite defeats inflicted on the Britons.**

Biscay coast, was the territory of the Pictones, or Pictavii. This name is a Roman label, referring to the 'painted' (i.e. tattooed) men of the area and does not reflect any kinship with the Picts of the British Isles. The Pictavii of Gaul were probably a collection of disparate tribes that had come together under a single confederation leader, and whose members may have had widely different origins. This disparity became apparent during the Gallic Wars, in which the leadership of the confederation sided with Rome while several thousand warriors went to join their Celtic cousins fighting against Caesar.

'THE STRAIN WAS MADE WORSE BY THE CELTS' HABIT OF TAUNTING THEIR ENEMIES.'

Despite this confused allegiance the Pictavii were rewarded for their loyalty to Rome and were granted additional territory. They had always been a seafaring people, and indeed had assisted Roman operations against the Veneti in 52 BCE by providing ships. With the Veneti crushed, the Pictavii became the dominant sea power on the Atlantic coast, trading with the British Isles and along the European coasts. The Pictavii managed to resist excessive Romanization despite borrowing much from Roman architecture and engineering.

Gallic Revolts

After pacifying the Belgae and annexing Armorica, Caesar engaged in what amounted to politico-military showboating for a time. In 55 BCE his army crossed the Rhine, supposedly to punish the Suebi for entering Gaul, and campaigned in Germania for a while. He then led a somewhat ill-planned incursion into Britain. The Britons' use of chariots was an unpleasant novelty for the Roman force, as chariots had not been seen on a European battlefield for many years.

Caesar's army returned to Britain the following year, 54 BCE, inflicting a defeat on the Catuvellauni tribe. This had no great significance; the Britons promised tribute but did not deliver it, and Rome was unable to enforce the requirement. However, all this activity enhanced Caesar's political reputation in Rome, which was his main aim.

RIGHT: Under the leadership of Ambiorix, the Eburones destroyed one Roman legion and besieged another in its fortified camp. A prompt response from Caesar's main force broke the siege after a pitched battle, after which a campaign to pacify the Belgae was undertaken.

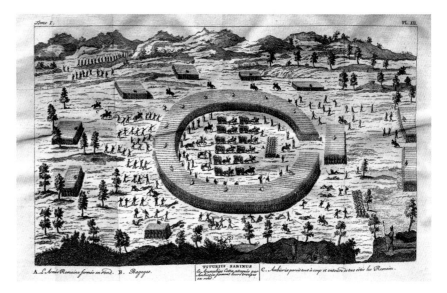

Exactly what Caesar might have done next is open to question, since events forced him to deal with a crisis in Gaul. Late in 54 BCE or early in 53 BCE, the Eburones, a tribe variously described as Gauls, Belgae or Germanic, rose up in revolt and annihilated the local Roman forces. This revolt was joined by the Nervii and others, requiring a hasty campaign by Caesar's force to restore the situation. Alongside the main campaign, Roman forces undertook several small punitive expeditions that seemed to bring the situation under control.

The relative peace lasted for most of 53 BCE, but by winter the Gauls were again in open conflict with Rome. This is often termed a revolt, as many tribes had agreements with Rome that were violated when they joined the fighting. Others had never accepted Roman dominance, so while some tribes were in revolt others were fighting against a perceived threat. In the end it made little difference – the Gauls rose against Rome under the leadership of Vercingetorix, a chieftain of the Averni.

Although the Averni were no longer as powerful as they had been they were still a major force in Gaulish politics. However, Vercingetorix was not the commander of a unified army but the leader of a force that had a common foe. His warriors were numerous but disorganized and prone to arguing among themselves. Some were willing to change allegiance if it suited them, thus the Gallic revolt was not a clear-cut 'us versus them'

situation. It was much more complex, creating cracks in the
Gaulish front that could be exploited by Rome and a situation
where some tribes were viewed with varying degrees of enmity.
Therefore some defeated tribes were allowed to return to
Roman allegiance with scarcely any censure while others were
savagely punished.

Scorched Earth Policy

Vercingetorix realized that the Roman weakness was the length
of its supply line, and implemented a 'scorched earth' policy to
deny Caesar adequate supplies. He also took steps to ensure that
his own forces could be adequately supplied and thus remain
concentrated wherever possible. His offensives were aimed at
Roman and pro-Roman settlements, with political as well as
military objectives. Vercingetorix was not merely concerned
with removing Roman bases and supporters, he hoped to inflict
defeats that would cause more tribes to join the fight or at least
remain neutral.

Gaulish warriors fought Roman troops and their allied
tribes in various places, but the decisive events of the
campaign played out between Vercingetorix and Caesar.
Vercingetorix besieged Gorgobina, a fortified settlement
of the Roman-allied Aedui tribe. This forced Caesar to
march to the city's relief, although his supply situation was
questionable. Vercingetorix abandoned the siege and went
to intercept the Roman force, fighting an unsuccessful
cavalry action at Noviodunum.

After this setback, Vercingetorix decided to draw out
the Roman force along its overstretched supply line.
He retired as the Romans advanced on Avaricum, then
harassed them as they besieged the city. Avaricum lay in
the lands of the Bituriges and was well defended, but could
not hold out forever. With the Roman siege progressing
and his own supply situation worsening, Vercingetorix
began to listen more to the urgings of his hot-headed allies.

Eventually giving in to demands for direct action,
Vercingetorix established a position close to the Roman
force and tried to tempt Caesar into attacking. When this

BELOW: Vercingetorix,
chieftain of the Averni,
fought a sophisticated
campaign, seeking
to deprive Caesar of
supplies and local
support. His strategy
was compromised by a
rash decision to fight the
Romans head-on.

failed, attacks against the Roman siege works were increased, but without success. Facing imminent assault the Gauls in Avaricum attempted a breakout. They were driven back into the town, which was subsequently stormed. The fall of Avaricum robbed Vercingetorix of a great many warriors, most of whom were put to the sword by the Roman attackers. It also gained Caesar's army a reprieve from a desperate supply situation, since the town contained large stocks of grain.

The political fallout from Avaricum was mixed. Caesar's forces made a series of rapid gains, attacking several Gaulish settlements in succession. This might have shaken Gaulish morale, but this was countered by Vercingetorix's reputation. He had argued against defending Avaricum and actually gained in stature for being right, which caused some wavering tribes to send men to join the fight. Even some previously pro-Roman tribes joined with their Celtic brethren in fighting for a free Gaul.

Caesar next advanced on Gergovia, capital of the Averni. The assault went badly, as Roman discipline broke down and the attacking force was repelled with heavy losses. Attacks on the Roman supply line and even more uprisings threatened Caesar's

BELOW: The surrender of Vercingetorix was a spectacle of dignity in defeat. From his horse he threw down his weapons at the feet of Caesar, symbolizing the submission of Gaul's proud warriors to a superior enemy.

army with isolation and annihilation. With no other options left Caesar concentrated his forces for a decisive action and hired Germanic mercenaries.

The resulting battle was fierce and somewhat confused, with cavalry from both sides clashing along the line of march. Eventually the Gauls were driven back and pursued, taking refuge in the city of Alesia. There, they were besieged as Caesar's force threw up a line of fortifications facing the town and another facing outwards to prevent relief.

The Battle of Alesia was characterized by Roman attempts to complete their siege works and Gaulish attacks to try to prevent them from doing so. Vercingetorix's cavalry managed to break through the Roman fortifications on the second attempt, joining other Gaulish warriors in the area. These launched a series of attacks on the Roman works, some of which coincided with breakout attempts. Although the Roman force was hard pressed, Caesar's ability to move reserves around allowed the siege to continue unbroken.

ABOVE: Glanum was conquered by Rome during Caesar's Gallic Wars, as this carving commemorates, and became a centre for Romanization of Gaul. It was the site of the first triumphal arch built in Gaul, but was destroyed in 260 AD as the Empire was in decline.

Despite a final, desperate breakout attempt Vercingetorix's army was unable to escape. A Roman counterattack on the relief force caused a collapse in morale, and many of the Gaulish warriors outside the walls drifted away. Vercingetorix and his men were left to their fate, and ultimately forced to surrender. Vercingetorix was taken as a captive to Rome and eventually executed.

A smaller revolt took place in 51 BCE, but this was over almost before it started and thereafter Gaul was very much a Roman possession. The consequences for Caesar and Rome were far-reaching but for the Gauls they were even greater. Although there were occasional revolts and other troubles, Gaul was gradually Romanized and remained part of the Empire until its final collapse centuries later.

8

THE CELTS IN THE BRITISH ISLES

The Celtic people of the British Isles are generally referred to as the Insular Celts, as opposed to the Continental Celts. However, the divide, if it existed at all, was not so clear-cut.

Geographical divisions did lead to some cultural variations, but there was movement of people, trade goods and ideas across the sea between Britain and the Continent throughout the Celtic era. The Insular Celts were not separate or isolated from their Continental cousins, and indeed in some cases they were close kin. Some tribes of the British Isles were closely related to Continental tribes, or formed from an offshoot of a tribe that migrated for whatever reason.

No map of the tribes of Britain can present the full picture, even as a snapshot of the situation at that time. Inter-tribal

OPPOSITE: **Perhaps the most famous of Celtic leaders in the British Isles was Boudica, who led an initially successful rebellion against Roman rule. The idea of a female leader was very alien to the Romans; being defeated by one was a severe blow to their pride.**

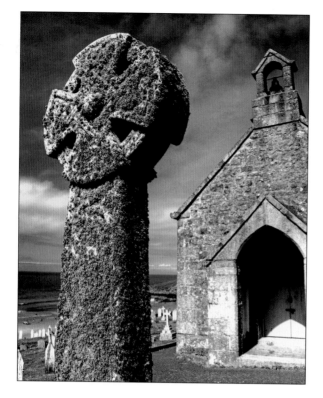

ABOVE: **The Insular Celts were subject to strong cultural influences first from Rome, then the arrival of Christianity.**

OPPOSITE: **By the period 800–900 CE, the culture of much of Britain had been altered by the influence of the Norsemen, or Vikings. Settlers and conquerors created 'Viking kingdoms' that mixed Norse culture with some Celtic influences.**

conflict caused territories to expand and shrink, and the influx of tribes moving away from Roman expansion caused even greater upheaval. Much of what we know about Celtic life and politics in Britain comes from Roman sources or mythological accounts passed down (and inevitably distorted) through the writings of later chroniclers. Thus any picture of Celtic Britain on a given day will be incomplete and based to some extent on scanty evidence and guesswork.

Celtic culture was subject to heavy Roman influences after the British Isles were invaded and partially conquered. However, the degree to which any given tribe was Romanized varied considerably, and often for differing reasons. By way of example the Dumnonii of the Cornwall-Devon region retained much of their culture, ironically perhaps, because they did not greatly resist the Roman incursion.

The Dumnonii were probably a loose tribal confederation that did not have unified leadership nor fortified places to defend. They apparently did not make use of coinage, and so might be thought primitive by some observers. However, they were able to carry on considerable trade with the tribes of Armorica across the English Channel. When the Romans arrived the Dumnonii probably lacked the central leadership required to present any significant resistance, and seem to have accepted the invasion once it became a fact of life. As a result of this fairly peaceable acquiescence the Dumnonii were not subject to large Roman garrisons nor major building projects to support them, and seem to have gone on with their lives much as before.

For the Dumnonii, at least, the Roman occupation of Britain came and went as just another chapter in a long history. However, Romanization did result in the development of an administrative centre at Dumnoniorum, or modern Exeter, and the creation of a ruling house that became extremely important

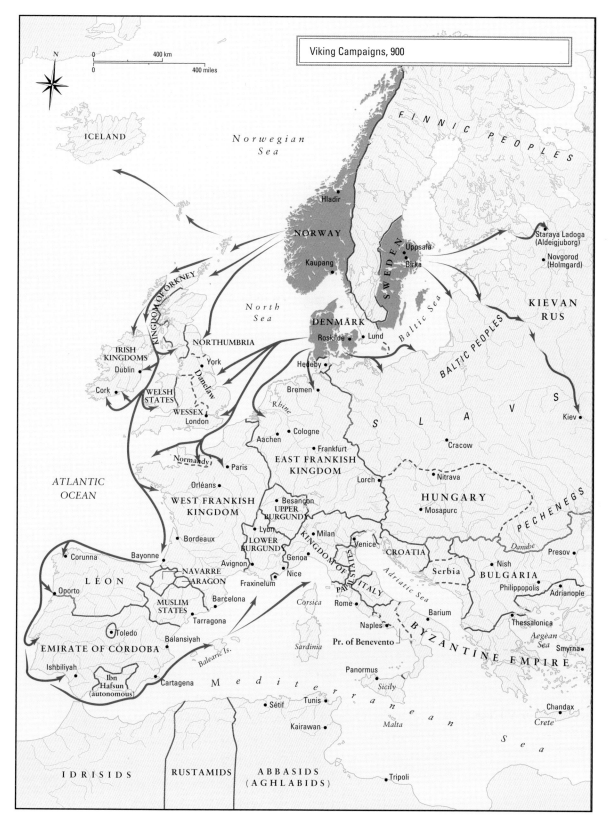

Viking Campaigns, 900

in British affairs after the fall of Rome. Among the real and legendary kings descended from the Dumnonii was King Arthur, who may have been based on one or more historical figures.

Celtic Britain

As previously noted there was no huge Celtic invasion of the British Isles. Instead there was an influx of migrating people who settled in various areas, and a gradual 'Celtization' of the existing population by intermarriage and the spreading of ideas. By the time of the first Roman incursions, most of Britain was thoroughly Celtic, with well-established tribes and tribal confederations controlling large areas. The degree of control over any given area depended largely on how centralized a given tribe was, and this could vary considerably.

BELOW: Tintagel castle, in the lands previously controlled by the Dumnonii, is traditionally the place where legendary King Arthur was conceived. Arthur's lineage could be traced back to the kings of the Dumnonii, whose existence derived from partial Romanization of the tribe.

The Trinovantes tribe of what is now Essex and Suffolk were one of the most powerful Celtic tribes in Britain at the time of Caesar's incursions in 55–54 BCE. They were at the time in conflict with the powerful Atrebates, and were not getting the best of it. Hearing about the possible Roman incursion from their Continental friends, the Trinovantes made a diplomatic approach to Julius Caesar, offering cooperation in the event of a Roman incursion. This was probably a smart move, as historically those Continental tribes that cooperated with Rome benefited considerably; those that resisted did not prosper.

Between Caesar's two expeditions the Trinovantes' king was killed and his dispossessed son Mandubracius went to Caesar for aid. During his second expedition Caesar reinstalled Mandubracius and admonished his enemies to desist. However, this arrangement had little in the way of teeth, and the promised tribute and hostages did not materialize.

The term 'king' in a Celtic context can have various meanings. Sometimes it is a label applied by historians or outside observers to describe a powerful leader whose role was similar to that of a king, but who was not one as such. Thus references to Celtic kings and queens should be treated with caution; Mandubracius was not a king in the same sense as a medieval monarch, and although the system of leadership and rulership varied from one tribe to another it remained an evolving version of the traditional Celtic way of life rather than the entrenched feudal system that might be inferred.

Be that as it may, powerful Celtic leaders who wielded the power of kings and queens did emerge in Britain. Power struggles involving the Trinovantes and their close relations the Catuvellauni and Cantici resulted in Cunobeline of the Catuvellauni becoming king of all three tribes. Cunobeline referred to himself explicitly as a king, using the Latin 'rex'. Cunobeline's power play was well timed, coming in 9 CE just after the destruction of three Roman legions in the Teutoberger forest by Germanic tribesmen.

With Rome distracted and her prestige plummeting, Cunobeline seized his moment and unified the three tribes under his rule. To do so he must have been well informed about foreign affairs, and astute enough to care about what was happening outside his immediate area of influence. This shows that the tribes of Britain were every bit as much an international power as the Greek city-states, Carthage or even early Rome had been. They were part of the wider picture and they knew it. However, international politics is a dangerous game in any era. Expansion of the Trinovantes eventually provided the pretext for the Roman invasion that conquered most of Britain.

In contrast to the centralized Trinovantes, the Durotriges tribal confederation was loosely organized, with no central dynasty or traditional leaders. They lived along the south coast, in what is now Devon and the surrounding area, probably in fairly small settlements grouped into minor tribes that loosely cooperated when necessary.

ABOVE: Romani influence may have been the cause of Celtic chieftains starting to refer to themselves as kings. These coins were issued by Cunobeline, who used the term Rex and is referred to by some historians as 'King of the Britons'.

ABOVE: **The Belgiae of Britain were probably migrants from the Continent. Some may have arrived in Britain before the Roman conquest of Gaul; others fled when their homelands were overrun and joined their kin in the British Isles.**

The Durotriges' way of life was in many ways what we have come to see as the 'standard' Celtic model, with some of the most impressive hill-forts still surviving to this day. The Durotriges were metalworkers and traders, mining their raw materials from local deposits and working them into trade goods. These went inland into Britain or across the Channel to Gaul, although the tribe does seem to have exported more than it imported. Unlike their westerly neighbours the Dumnonii, the Durotriges vigorously opposed Roman incursions and were forcibly incorporated into the Empire.

Continental Migrations

The Belgiae are noted by Roman writers as counting among the British tribes, but given that their name was used as a label for tribes in a particular part of Gaul, it seems likely that this group was of Belgian origin. Exactly which tribe they came from is an open question; it is most probable that the British Belgiae originated from several Continental tribes. If so, then their presence in Britain would be a result of migrations to escape Roman advances, and the British Belgiae would have been a new tribe or tribal group formed by fragments of other tribes displaced from their ancestral homes.

Roman sources place the Belgiae around Venta Belgarum, now Winchester. It is not clear if this territory was won by conquest, settled by agreement or even granted by Roman administrators. The practice of placing tribes where they would best serve Roman interests was well established, and even if the Belgiae were not pro-Rome they could serve as a distraction for other local tribes, making them less likely to oppose Roman interests.

Similarly, the Cantiaci tribe, from whom their home territory of Kent takes its name, was probably formed when migrants from Gaul joined with people already living in the area to form a new tribe. The Cantiaci had much in common with the Gaulish Celts, notably their methods of burial, which suggests that the migrants brought European customs with them.

The Atrebates were another migrant tribe. Their name translates as 'settlers', and it seems that the tribe, or parts of it, migrated across Europe and settled in Gaul, Belgium and the British Isles. The Atrebates of the British Isles retained strong links with their cousins among the Belgae of the Continent and may have sheltered key members of the Belgian Atrebates tribe when their war with Rome went badly.

> 'BRITAIN REMAINED A STRONGHOLD FOR "GAULS" WHO HAD NOT SUBMITTED TO ROME.'

The Atrebates were extremely powerful in the British Isles just before the Roman invasion, and, as was often the case with powerful neighbours, Rome approached the tribe diplomatically. As a result the Atrebates benefited from friendship with Rome in the early years of the first century CE, and looked to Rome for assistance when they came under pressure from the Catuvellauni. When his tribe was overrun by the Catuvellauni, the last king of the Atrebates, Verica, took refuge in Rome and appealed for aid. This gave Roman Emperor Claudius a pretext for an invasion of Britain, starting in 43 CE.

Roman Invasions

The initial 'invasions' of Britain, conducted by Julius Caesar as part of his Gallic Wars, were really little more than demonstrations of his power to the political arena back home. They had little lasting effect – even the agreement to hand over tribute and hostages was not honoured by British tribes. Britain remained a stronghold for 'Gauls' who had not submitted to Rome and who remained a threat, but bringing the islands under Roman control would be a big task.

Three invasions were planned between 34 and 25 BCE, but were cancelled for various reasons, mainly a need to deal with crises elsewhere in the Empire. In 40 CE, Emperor Caligula led an army to the Channel coast, but this was more about his personal lunacy than any concrete plans for invasion. However, some of the preparations made by Caligula proved useful when war between the Atrebates and the Catuvellauni gave Rome new impetus to invade the British Isles.

In 43 CE, a Roman force of four legions sailed from the Continent and landed in Britain. There is some confusion in Roman accounts as to where they landed and where the Britons gave battle, but after some skirmishing the Celts were pushed back and the Roman forces marched inland. A decisive clash came in the lands of the Cantiaci tribe, probably on the River Medway.

The resulting action is now normally called the Battle of the Medway, although the exact spot is not known. It was a hard-fought affair that went on over two days as the Britons tried to prevent a Roman crossing of the river. A crossing was eventually forced by the heavily armed Romans, and the Celtic force was driven back to make another stand on the Thames.

The Celts were led in these battles by Togodumnus and Caratacus of the Catuvellauni. Both survived the actions on the Medway and the Thames, although the Celtic army was heavily defeated there and many warriors were lost when they were pursued into the Essex marshes. Togodumnus died soon afterward, and his exhausted, demoralized tribe surrendered without much more fighting. Caratacus survived and fled to Wales where he continued to resist the invasion.

Over the next four years, Roman forces campaigned in the south-eastern corner of Britain, gaining control over territory south-east of a line between the Humber and Severn rivers. Pushing into Wales proved more of a problem, however.

The Roman campaign opened in 48 CE with an advance into the territory of the Deceangli, who made little or no

BELOW: The exact location of the Battle of the Medway is difficult to pinpoint, and may not have been near the site of this modern memorial. The outcome of the battle is well known though; it was a severe defeat for the Britons.

resistance. With the northeastern corner of Wales thus pacified, Roman forces pushed into the territory of the Silures. The latter were a fairly loose tribal confederation with no centralized leadership, which gave Caratacus the opportunity to act as their war-leader.

Caratacus

Under the leadership of Caratacus, the Silures put up a spirited resistance. Engagements varied from small hit-and-run raids and general harassment to full-scale battles, with their guerrilla tactics being particularly effective. Roman authorities became seriously alarmed at the level of threat posed by the Silures, and even after Caratacus moved to the Ordovices, whose lands were to the north, the Silures continued to resist.

Indeed, the Silures went on fighting against Rome long after Caratacus' eventual defeat. The Roman invaders tried one of their standard strategies, establishing forts to operate from in Silurian territory, but the units sent to construct them became isolated and surrounded, and were only extricated with great difficulty. In 52 CE the Silures inflicted a serious defeat on the Second Legion, which was at the time counted among the best units Rome had available.

Around 78 CE, the Silures ceased fighting against Rome, although there are few details as to how this happened. The Roman historian Tacitus records that it was not possible to sway the Silures from their chosen course of action by either kindness or cruelty, but does not say how their decision to accept Roman rule came about. We can only assume that after more than 20 years of war, it suited the Silures to make peace. This decision was likely made on their own terms and to suit their own interests; they had well proven that they were not interested in anyone else's agenda.

ABOVE: During the Romano-British era, Tre'r Ceiri hillfort grew from a small settlement of about 100 people to a fairly major town, with at least 150 dwellings and over 400 inhabitants. With its own water supply, the fort was a formidable stronghold.

ABOVE: **The Menai Massacre removed the druids as a rallying point for Celtic resistance against Rome, and not coincidentally wiped out generations of oral histories. To some extent, the attack was a strike against the very identity of the Celtic Britons.**

In the meantime, Caratacus joined the Ordovices, and in 50 or 51 CE was defeated at the Battle of Caer Caradoc. Caratacus had excelled in guerrilla fighting but in a straight pitched battle Roman equipment and discipline tended to win out. In an effort to even the odds, Caratacus drew up his force on high ground behind a river, and further strengthened his position with hasty field fortifications. Despite a shower of missiles from the Celts on high ground, Roman troops forced a crossing of the river and penetrated the defensive line, advancing uphill to engage the Celts hand-to-hand.

With his army defeated, Caratacus was forced to flee again. He took refuge with the Brigantes of the Pennines, but they were less inclined to stand against Rome and surrendered him. Taken to Rome, he was to have been executed as part of the Triumph celebrating his defeat, but gave a speech that persuaded the emperor to spare him. The gist of this speech was that the glory of Rome was enhanced by victory over such worthy opponents as Caratacus and his people, and he had a point. The Triumph was well earned; Caratacus was one of Rome's most persistent and successful enemies, and defeating him was rightly described as one of the greatest victories won by any Roman commander.

In the meantime, the pacification of Wales continued. Around 60 CE a Roman campaign reached the druidic centre on the isle of Mona (Anglesey) and destroyed it. In what has since become known as the Menai Massacre, much of the druidic tradition of the Celts was eliminated, resulting in an enormous loss of historical knowledge as well as druidic lore. To the Romans, the elimination of the druids was probably little more than a politico-military stratagem intended to remove a rallying point against their occupation. To the Celts it was more like the murder of a culture.

Revolts in Britain

The Iceni tribe of what is now Norfolk and the surrounding area was formed of several smaller tribes. A wealthy and powerful tribe, the Iceni had some diplomatic conflict with Julius Caesar's expeditions but chose not to oppose Roman advances into Britain. The tribe became a more or less autonomous ally of Rome once south eastern Britain had been pacified, and had relatively slight – and generally cordial – dealings with the invaders for many years.

That changed when the tribal king, Prasutagus, died. His will left his holdings jointly to the Roman emperor and his daughters, which was presumably unacceptable to Rome. Roman attitudes to women wielding power over anything other than a kitchen or perhaps a shopping list were rather negative, so perhaps the annexation of the Iceni was prompted by outrage. Perhaps it was simple opportunism, but whatever the reason the Iceni were treated as if they had been conquered in warfare.

It is recorded that Prasutagus' wife Boudica was flogged and his daughters raped. There is some doubt over what that actually means, as the Roman definition of rape was 'to carry off by force'. The daughters might have been forcibly taken as hostages, or may have been physically raped (or both). Either way, this treatment by the Iceni's former friends resulted in a violent revolt.

Joined by the Trinovantes and other tribes, the Iceni rose up and attacked Camulodunum, which had become a Roman settlement. The Roman governor of Britain was campaigning in the west and could not immediately bring his forces into action to quell the revolt. An attempt by elements of the 9th Legion to intervene was soundly defeated – Tacitus records that all of the infantry were killed but the cavalry were able to withdraw.

The Iceni attacked Londinium (London) and Verulamium (St Albans) before they were brought to battle by the main Roman force in Britain. Although outnumbered and forced to fight after a long march from Wales, the legions chose their ground well, limiting how many of the large British force could come at them at once.

Boudica's address to her tribe before the battle reflected some of the key values of Celtic society. Men might squabble and fight over trivialities but once the women of the tribe were involved, things got deadly serious. She spoke to her followers as a woman and a mother wronged, and also as a warrior leader who was determined to live or die free.

'HAD THE REVOLT GONE ON FOR LONGER, BRITISH HISTORY MIGHT HAVE BEEN VERY DIFFERENT.'

The Britons were numerous and highly motivated, but they were disorganized. After the initial assaults were repelled the Romans went on the offensive. Here, British tactics were their undoing. As other tribes had done before (and with more success) the Iceni and their allies had positioned their supplies and their families in a line of wagons close to the battlefield. On occasions these not-quite-noncombatants had acted as a bulwark to shelter a defeated force or a refuge to rally in. This time, however, they prevented a retreat.

Iceni Defeated

This inability to break off as the battle turned against them ensured that the defeat of the Iceni was decisive. Had the revolt gone on for longer, British history might have been very different; the Roman emperor actually considered retreating from Britain during the revolt, but its suppression instead paved the way for further expansion northwards. The fate of Boudica herself remains unclear – some accounts say she poisoned herself rather than submit to Rome, others that she became ill and died soon after the defeat of her army.

In the years immediately following Boudica's revolt, several other tribes attempted to throw off Roman rule, or moved from a generally pro-Roman position to a rather less friendly one. Among them were the Brigantes whose territory centred on the Pennines. The Brigantes were a large tribal federation that had been generally positive towards Rome. The king of the Brigantes, Venutius, was staunchly anti-Roman in his views, but his wife Cartimundia held the opposite view and it was she that the tribe followed. Thus, in 51 CE, when Caratacus fled his defeat in Wales and came to the Brigantes for support, Cartimundia handed him over to the Romans.

Friendship with Rome was beneficial to the Brigantes' position, and Venutius' opposition became sufficiently tiresome that some time after 51 CE, Cartimundia threw him out, too, and married again. Venutius formented revolts against both Cartimundia and Rome, which were put down by joint Brigantes-Roman action. In 69 CE, taking advantage of the chaos in Rome caused by the Year of Four Emperors, Venutius launched another revolt and managed to gain control of the Brigantes.

The Brigantes thus became staunch opponents of Rome, and conflict went on for many years. Possibly triggered or encouraged by the resistance of the Brigantes, other tribes also rebelled against Rome, or carried on resisting longer than they might have if they were fighting in isolation.

ABOVE: The defeat of the Iceni was overwhelming. Unable to retreat, the tribe's warriors were forced to fight on long after any chance of victory was gone and were massacred. Boudica herself is claimed to have taken poison rather than submit to Rome.

Caledonia

In 78 CE, Britain received a new Roman governor, Agricola. Much of what we know about the Celts of Britain comes from

ABOVE: According to Tacitus, the leader of the Caledones was Calgacus. He records a rousing speech given by Calgacus to his warriors before the Battle of Mons Graupius, but does not reveal how he came to know what the Caledones' leader said.

the account of Agricola's career written by his son-in-law, Tacitus. Agricola carried out a series of campaigns in Britain from 78–84 CE, some of which were aimed at pacifying revolts. He also defeated the Brigantes and pushed north into Caledonia. Among the tribes Agricola encountered were the Votadini, whose name meant 'fort dwellers'. Not only did their territory, which stretched from north of the Brigantes to the banks of the Forth, contain a great many hill-forts but they also built fortifications around many smaller settlements including farming hamlets.

Relatively little is known about the tribes of Caledonia, largely because they successfully resisted Roman conquest. The most important tribe of the region was known to the Romans as the Caledones or Caledonii. The context of this name seems to vary – at times it refers to a single tribe or tribal confederation, at others it is used in the same manner as the term 'Gaul' to mean anyone living in what the Romans called Caledonia.

Despite setting up forts to support the campaign, Agricola was unable to conquer the Caledones and had difficulty in bringing them to a decisive battle. He apparently succeeded in doing so at a place known as Mons Graupius, although the location remains unclear. According to Tacitus, the Caledonians were led by a man named Calgacus and made use of chariots, infantry and missile troops, while the Romans sent forward only their auxiliary forces. The Caledonians were heavily defeated but retired through woods that confounded the Roman pursuit, rendering the expensive victory indecisive.

Although the Caledonians allegedly suffered heavy casualties, they remained independent and determined to resist Roman rule. Further Roman incursions were met by guerrilla tactics rather than a pitched battle, and ultimately Caledonia proved to lie beyond the reach of the Roman Empire. A chain of forts was constructed along Gask Ridge in what is now Perthshire to secure the frontier against the Caledones. Although for a time Rome still paid lip service to the idea of conquering Caledonia, the construction of Hadrian's Wall (122–130 CE) and the Antonine Wall (142–144 CE) were a physical declaration that the 'Gauls' of Caledonia would remain free of Rome.

Those 'Gauls' were the subject of admiration for many Romans. Tacitus records his belief that the Caledones could never be conquered because they did not understand when they were beaten. He suggests that so long as half a dozen warriors remained they would fight on and believe themselves invincible. Tacitus also expresses admiration for the 'Gauls' of Britain, noting their virtues and commenting that they were every bit as noble as the Gauls of the Continent used to be… before Rome conquered them.

These sentiments aside, the Caledonian tribes halted the Roman incursion and offered such persistent harassment to any attempt to take territory in Caledonia that the Roman Empire built its first fortified border along Gask Ridge. The policies of Emperor Hadrian, who implemented a fortification programme along the borders, came later. In this, Gask Ridge in Caledonia represented perhaps a high water mark in the expansion of the Roman Empire. As with the tribes of Germania, the Celts of Caledonia forced the Empire to settle for trying to keep them out rather than forcibly bringing them in.

Agricola returned southward after 84 CE, and although there were various expeditions for a time Rome was willing to leave Caledonia alone. A renewed attempt at conquest of the lowlands began around 140 CE, with Roman forces campaigning

BELOW: Emperor Hadrian's policy of building permanent fortifications along the borders of the Empire was a tacit admission that the Germanic and Caledonian tribes would never be conquered. Expeditions into Caledonia continued for a time but even the Antonine Wall ultimately proved untenable.

against the Damnonii in the west and the Votadini and Selgovae in the east. Sufficient progress was made to permit the building of the Antonine Wall, but despite repeated forays and expeditions by Roman troops the region north of the walls remained largely unknown and most definitely unconquered.

The Antonine Wall was abandoned in the 150s, then reoccupied and abandoned again within a few years. After this, there was no serious Roman threat to Caledonia. Trade went on across the buffer zone around the wall, and tribes in the area became somewhat Romanized. Those further south were subject to even greater influences, not just from Rome but also from all the cultures that made up and existed around the fringes of the Roman Empire.

Roman troops were withdrawn from much of Britain in 383 CE and left the islands completely around 410 CE. Their departure did not, however, allow a sudden resurgence of Celtic culture. Years of occupation and membership of the Empire had altered the Celts of Britain into something else, something that can perhaps best be described as Romano-Britons. It was these Britons that faced the invasions of Germanic tribes from the continent and the depredations of raiders from Scandinavia, to eventually emerge as the modern population of Britain.

By this time, Christianity had also gained a foothold in the British Isles. Its spread was sporadic and at times painful, with reversions to paganism and other troubles along the way. Wales was an early stronghold of Christianity, with Scotland being gradually converted in the fifth and sixth centuries. This gave the British Church a distinctly Celtic flavour, with many myths and historical figures being co-opted into the new faith.

Celtic-Christians helped spread the new faith throughout England, despite many setbacks, and brought their unique style of

BELOW: Hadrian's wall was backed by a chain of heavily garrisoned forts, making its 73-mile length one of the most strongly fortified frontiers in history. The wall zone became a zone of interaction between the independent tribes of Caledonia and the Romano-Britons to the south.

decoration to their new holy buildings. By the end of the seventh century most of Britain was Christian. This was a highly influential factor in historical events thereafter, and forms part of the Celtic legacy that helped shape modern British culture – which has in turn influenced the development of other cultures wordwide.

Ireland and the Celtic Legacy

Ireland remained beyond the reach of the Roman Empire, so there is little in the way of historical record for the Celts of Ireland – other, of course, than the mythology already discussed. This mythology doubtless has its origins in historical fact, but unravelling the truth is problematic.

The general picture of the Irish Celts is one of proud and warlike people, who raided and feuded with one another on a frequent basis. They also interacted with the Celts of Europe and the rest of the British Isles, with some tribes crossing between Wales, Ireland and Scotland to find new homes or to escape their enemies.

Prior to the arrival of Christianity in Ireland, and with it a literate group who could record the myths and histories of the Irish people, the only form of writing available was Ogham. This writing dates from at least the fourth century CE and probably somewhat earlier. Its alphabet consists of simple vertical, horizontal and diagonal strokes that are easy to carve into wood or stone with a sharp object, and it is in this form that Ogham writing has survived.

Ogham is mainly found on monuments in Ireland but also in Wales, the Isle of Man and parts of England and Scotland. Short inscriptions are the norm, although there is some evidence that it might have been used for accounting and similar purposes. Ogham writing is not suitable for lengthy histories, however, so no detailed records of the pre-literacy era have survived in this form.

ABOVE: **The withdrawal of Roman forces from Britain left behind a culture that had been significantly changed over the years of occupation. Further upheaval lay ahead, not least due to incursions by Germanic and Scandinavian peoples.**

ABOVE: **The prevalence of fortified homesteads and small settlements in Ireland speaks of a violent and turbulent history. Much of the low-level conflict that went on was unrecorded; only major events found their way into mythology and survived long enough to be chronicled.**

Although early events in Ireland remain unclear, five kingdoms emerged: Ulster, Connaught, Mide, Leinster and Munster. Their fortunes varied, with territories won and lost. Events of some of the Irish myths are partially corroborated by the existence of battle sites, towns or fortifications on the sites described, although of course many details have become distorted. However, the traditional Celtic myths are in many cases the best or only guide to the early history of Ireland.

War between Connaught in the north-west and Ulster in the north-east seems to have been very frequent. Connacht was, according to early myths, a homeland of the Fir Bolgs. The Fir Bolgs were allowed to retain Connaught even after the Milesians arrived and took control of Ireland. As with many such myths, there are references to invasions and conflicts that probably have their origins in fact. Various attempts have been made to correlate these events with migrations of tribes from elsewhere in the British Isles or from the Continent, but it has not proven easy to find a connection between oft-retold and revised myths and actual events – which may themselves never have been documented.

The kingdom of Mide emerged in the first century CE. Its territory included the hill of Tara, which had mythological significance as well as being the seat of the High Kings of Ireland. The institution of High Kings is a complex one, inasmuch as being High King did not equate to rulership over all of Ireland. Those records that survive show that succession to the position was sometimes dynastic but often took place for reasons that are not recorded. Some of these incidents may have been a result of violence or the shifting allegiance of tribes.

The Irish myths suggest that the position of High King could be tenuous, and that sometimes the power of the High King was eclipsed by that of other tribal leaders or kings, or even the commander of the High King's supposedly loyal warband. It seems that the High King was mostly a figurehead, and although he had power over his own people this was as their king, not as the High King.

Leinster in Eastern Ireland was, according to legend, ruled by a Fir Bolg tribe, until the fifth century. These people, known as Fir Dumnonii, may be associated with the Dumnonii of Devon and Cornwall. Leinster had dealings with mainland Britain long before its history began to be recorded, and after the departure from Britain of Roman forces, settlers from Leinster migrated into Anglesey and Wales. The Kingdom of Munster, in the south-west of Ireland, is also associated with the Fir Bolg people of myth, and was likely to be the point of arrival for many migrants crossing the sea northwards from Iberia. It is also possible that some of the Belgae settled in this region.

> 'ALTHOUGH EARLY EVENTS IN IRELAND REMAIN UNCLEAR, FIVE KINGDOMS EMERGED.'

Vikings in Ireland

Conflicts between these kingdoms were further complicated by the arrival of Viking settlers and raiders from 795 CE onwards. The Vikings settled along the coasts of Ireland and became part of the political landscape on a local level rather than as a unified group – much like the Irish themselves. Vikings became embroiled in Irish political conflicts as allies and enemies;

sometimes they sided with an Irish kingdom or tribe, sometimes attempts were made to oust them.

It did not prove possible to get rid of the Vikings, and along with those engaged in spreading the Christian faith they created new links with the outside world. Vikings in Ireland retained strong links with their cousins in Jorvik (York), for example, and this drew the Irish into their dealings as well. At the same time, Irish monks took the Word of God out into the wider world. They brought back new ideas from the Continent and the British Isles, and these too found their way into Irish society.

By this time the 'Celtic Era' was largely over. The world had changed and those changes filtered into Ireland. The Celtic influence remained strong, especially in terms of language and some customs, and as Celtic-descended people spread out across the wider world they took with them their art, culture and language. Hard times in Ireland and Scotland caused large numbers of Celts and Gaels to migrate to the New World where they both created enclaves of a shared heritage and influenced the development of emerging cultures in the Americas.

Although Roman occupation, the coming of Christianity and incursions by Germanic, Nordic and other tribes changed Celtic culture in Europe, it could not eradicate it. When Roman troops left Britain they left an evolved culture based on Celtic society tempered by new ideas from elsewhere. When the Vikings arrived in Ireland they became part of a new, evolving culture that would eventually become medieval Ireland, and would endure long after the end of the 'Viking Era'. In mainland Europe the Celts merged and melded into new societies

BELOW: The arrival of Viking raiders and settlers in Ireland did not result in 'Viking kingdoms' as in some other areas. Instead it simply created more factions in an already turbulent society.

that retained some of their values and forgot others.

The 'Celtic Era', if such a thing can be neatly defined, was a long one, and it was a period of great change that influenced everything that came afterward. Elements of the Hallstatt and La Tène cultures found their way, filtered through many generations and changing circumstances, to the Celtic Churches of Scotland, to the hilltop stone crosses of Ireland and to the industrial cities of the Americas.

In 410 CE, Roman Emperor Honorius told the Britons to look to their own defence, and so they did. Through many difficult centuries and numerous invasions by other people, the descendants of the Celts continued to survive and adapt. Their culture has evolved and become distorted over time, but then the culture of the Celts themselves was a distorted, evolved form of earlier societies. That process is still going on today.

Some elements of what we today think of as 'Celtic' culture might be unrecognizable to a smith creating new-fangled iron tools at Hallstatt, or to a Gaulish warrior setting off to fight against the Roman legions, but that is the nature of all cultures. Nothing stands still, and what we imagine a culture looked and felt like is at best merely a snapshot of how it was on one day in one place.

The Celtic culture was varied and rich, and their influence endures in place names, art, music, folk tales and traditional myths as well as languages still spoken and borrowed words still used. In a wider sense, Celtic culture channeled the development of society and religion in ways that we cannot begin to fathom, and through them it has influenced world events to this day.

ABOVE: **The major Celtic tribes of the British Isles retained their identities for a time , but ultimately the 'Celtic Era' came to an end. Eventually the tribal map would be replaced with one showing early kingdoms, and ultimately the realms of the medieval period.**

BIBLIOGRAPHY

Alcock, L 2003 *Kings and Warriors Craftsmen and Priests in Northern Britain AD 550-850*, Society of Antiquaries of Scotland

Aldhouse-Green, M 2004 *An archaeology of images: iconology and cosmology in Iron Age and Roman Europe.* Routledge

Armit, I 1997 *Celtic Scotland.* Batsford

Bradley, R 2007 *The Prehistory of Britain and Ireland.* Cambridge University Press

Caesar, Caius Julius (2010) *De Bello Gallico and Other Commentaries* HardPress Publishing

Chadwick, Nora Kershaw (1970) *The Celts.* Penguin Books

Collis, J 2003 *The Celts: origins, myths & inventions.* Tempus

Cunliffe, Barry, (1997) *The Ancient Celts.* Oxford University Press

Cunliffe, B 2004 *Iron Age Britain.* English Heritage

Ellis, Peter Berresford (2002) *Celtic Myths and Legends.* Running Press

Fraser, J 2009 *Caledonia to Pictland: Scotland to AD 795.* Edinburgh University Press

Gardner, JP and Handford, SA. (1983) *The Conquest of Gaul* Penguin Classics

Harding, D 2007 *The Archaeology of Celtic Art*, Routledge: Abingdon/New York.

Haywood, John (2001). *Atlas of the Celtic World* London Thames & Hudson Ltd.

Jackson, Kenneth Hurlstone (1971). *A Celtic Miscellany.* Penguin Classics

James, S 1999 *The Atlantic Celts: ancient people or modern invention?* British Museum

McNeill, John T. (1974) *The Celtic Churches: A History A. D. 200 to 1200.* University of Chicago Press

MacBain, Alexander (1976). *Celtic Mythology and Religion.* Folcroft Library Editions.

Müller, F 2009 *Art of the Celts 700BC – AD700.* Historisches Museum Bern

Potrebica, H. (1998) *Some Remarks on the Contacts Between the Greek and the Hallstatt Culture Considering the Area of Northern Croatia in the Early Iron Age.* Archaeopress

Rolleston, TW (2011) *Myths and Legends of the Celtic Race* Amazon Digital Services

Sjoestedt, Marie-Louise (2000) *Celtic Gods and Heroes* Dover Publications

INDEX